Physical Characteristics of the Saluki

(from the American Kennel

D1031873

Loin and Back: Back fairly broad, muscles slightly arched over loin.

Tail: Long, set on low and carried naturally in a curve.

Hindquarters: Strong, hipbones set well apart and stifle moderately bent, hocks low to the ground.

Coat: Smooth and of a soft silky texture.

Feet: Of moderate length, toes long and well arched...strong and supple and well feathered between the toes.

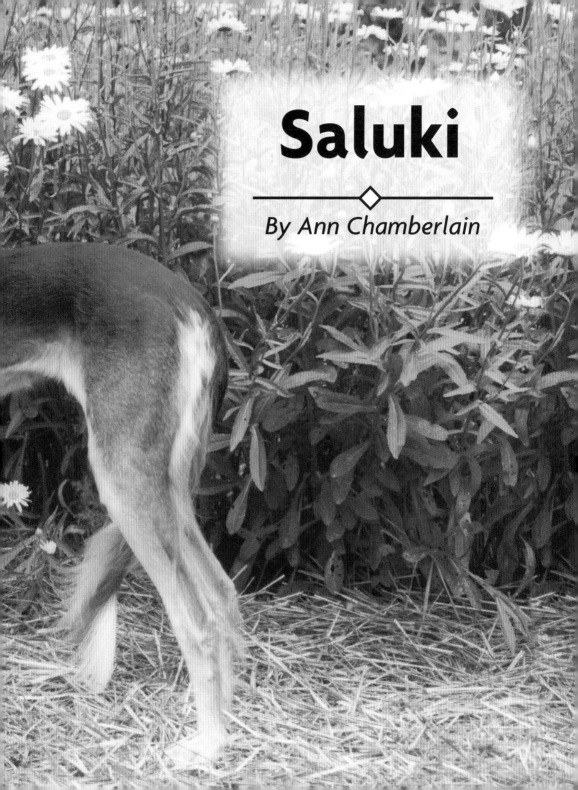

Saluki

◇

By Ann Chamberlain

Contents

Training Your Saluki **96**

Begin with the basics of training the puppy and adult dog. Learn the principles of house-training the Saluki, including the use of crates and basic scent instincts. Get started by introducing the pup to his collar and leash and progress to the basic commands. Find out about obedience classes and other activities.

Healthcare of Your Saluki **121**

By Lowell Ackerman DVM, DACVD
Become your dog's healthcare advocate and a well-educated canine keeper. Select a skilled and able veterinarian. Discuss pet insurance, vaccinations and infectious diseases, the neuter/spay decision and a sensible, effective plan for parasite control, including fleas, ticks and worms.

Showing Your Saluki **146**

Step into the center ring and find out about the world of showing pure-bred dogs. Here's how to get started in AKC shows, how they are organized and what's required for your dog to become a champion. Take a leap into the realms of obedience trials, agility, tracking, lure-coursing events and racing.

KENNEL CLUB BOOKS® **SALUKI**
ISBN: 1-59378-300-0

Copyright © 2005 • Kennel Club Books, LLC
308 Main Street, Allenhurst, New Jersey USA
Cover Design Patented: US 6,435,559 B2 • Printed in South Korea

Photography by Isabelle Français, Frank Powers, Steve Surfman, Karen Taylor, Michael Trafford and Alice van Kempen.
with additional photographs by:

Mary Bloom, Paulette Braun, T.J. Calhoun, Alan and Sandy Carey, Carolina Biological Supply, A. Jemolo, Carol Ann Johnson, Bill Jonas, Könemann Verlagsgesellschaft mbH, Köln, Dr. Dennis Kunkel, Tam C. Nguyen, Phototake, Jean Claude Revy, Alice Roche and Kent Standerford.

Illustrations by Patricia Peters.

The publisher wishes to thank all of the owners of the dogs featured in this book, including Helen Onto-Murphy, Frank & Winnie Powers, Joe & Pat Reese and Vickie Woods.

The origin of the Saluki is cloaked in mystery, legend and folktales. The breed, or the group of breeds very similar, has been recorded since the time of the Egyptian pharaohs.

SALUKI

ORIGIN OF THE SALUKI
Gift of Allah, Ancient of Ancients, El Hor, Al-Hurr, The Noble One. All of these phrases are used to describe the Saluki, a very ancient breed associated with nomadic tribes of the Near and Middle East, southwestern Asia and northern Africa. Today the Saluki is described as a separate breed, but I prefer to discuss the group of dogs that I would like to refer to as the "Saluki Complex." There are many so-called "breeds" that resemble one another, originating from such diverse areas as the republics of the former USSR to the northwestern coast of Africa, even into the southern reaches of Africa, that it is obvious that the Saluki type has been known since time immemorial. Clearly, this dog was associated with man from the very beginning, although there are very interesting theories as to who domesticated whom! Some recent proposals put forth have indicated that the social lives of wolves and man interacted in such a way that one could almost say that wolves domesticated man! The concept of an "Alpha"

Anubis, Egyptian god of death, has been represented as a Saluki-like dog with erect ears. This painted wooden statue is dated c. 300 BC.

figure seems to have contributed to the co-dependence between man and dog. Once the Alpha dog became subservient to the Alpha human, the dog-human connection was forged.

The dog became the companion and servant of man, bringing down game and herding cattle, goats and sheep. In return, the dog received warmth from the fire, the occasional "treat" and the love of the human family. The characteristics that set the Saluki Complex apart from the true herding and working breeds was their independence and ability to work without human intervention. They are all "coursing" hounds, whatever the prey. A coursing hound is distinguished from the other hounds by several characteristics. First of all, they are built to run long distances at great speed. Secondly, they have enough length of muzzle to grab and hold prey, either by the leg or by the throat. Thirdly, they rely on their remarkable eyesight to course the prey, never taking their eyes off the target animal. Of course, they come equipped with noses, too, and they use them! No dog will run around in the desert or forest just hoping to come across an animal to chase by sight. Noses first, then eyes! But once the prey is sighted, it is "all eyes."

The burial chamber of Pashedu, dated c. 1200 BC, is guarded by two Anubis dogs.

The actual history of the Saluki and related dogs is lost in time. Every member breed of this complex claims that the Egyptian paintings and bas reliefs depict "their" breed. What we actually see are ubiquitous sighthounds chasing gazelle in the desert.

Various early works of art have been considered as representing Salukis, with varying degrees of plausibility. Among the more convincing are the very small images on some stamp seals from Tepe Gawra in Mesopotamia, about 4000–3700 BC, and paintings and sculpture from the tomb of Tutankhamen, about 1450 BC. There are some earlier images of drop-eared hounds in Egyptian art, which may be autochthonous or may reflect Mesopotamian artistic conventions or even have been the work of Mesopotamian craftsmen.

The treatise of Arian, 139 AD, concerns coursing with what he describes as "Celtic" hounds, known to the Romans as *vertragi* in derivation from their original Celtic name. These seem perhaps to have been proto-Greyhounds rather than Salukis.

There are a number of rather realistic representations of Salukis, both smooth and feathered, in European paintings of the late medieval and Renaissance periods. Perhaps those were descendants of ones brought back by the Crusaders, or perhaps they

Representation of the nocturnal voyage of the Egyptian sun god, in a boat pulled by four Anubis dogs, while four cobra snakes pray. The Apophis snake is attacking the boat. Animals figure heavily in Egyptian pre-Christian history.

The word "Saluki" written in Arabic. The word is often pronounced "slu-ghi."

reflected continued trade contacts with the Muslim world.

None of this is necessarily conclusive evidence, but a "best guess" would be that Salukis have existed since at least 4000 BC, perhaps much longer. The Tepe Gawra images have exactly the same body proportions as a good modern Saluki, the tribal hound type rather than the show variety.

One Egyptian painting and one carving from about 3000 BC each depict a drop-eared dog with a ridge. To date, the breeds in this "complex" include the Sloughi, Azawakh, Pharaoh Hound, Greyhound, Afghan Hound, Persian Greyhound, Chart Polski, Chertaya, Khalag Tazy, Taigan, Bakhmul, Galgo Español, Magyar Agar, Caravan Hound and Rampuri, to name a few! The Rhodesian Ridgeback is never considered a part of this group by the Saluki people, but there are

strong indications that Saluki-type dogs did occur in southern Africa prior to the 16th century. Mummified remains of ridged Saluki-type dogs have been found buried along the banks of rivers in Botswana. Of the first three Sloughis imported into Holland in the early 1900s, depicted in Hutchinson's *Encyclopedia of Dogs*, two are ridged!

So, where to begin? The history of the Saluki as we know it today began with the first British adventurers who traveled to the Near and Middle East. Although apparently a few Salukis were brought back to Europe during the Middle Ages, it

CANIS LUPUS

"Grandma, what big teeth you have!" The gray wolf, *Canis lupus*, a familiar figure in fairy tales and legends, has had its reputation tarnished and its population pummeled over the centuries. Yet it is the descendants of this much-feared creature to which we open our homes and hearts. Our beloved dog, *Canis domesticus*, derives directly from the gray wolf, a highly social canine that lives in elaborately structured packs. In the wild, the gray wolf can range from 60 to 175 pounds, standing between 25 and 40 inches in height.

Front (LEFT) and back (RIGHT) sides of a slate, carved between 6000-5000 BC, depicting Salukis hunting gazelle.

A scene from the wall of the tomb of Rekh-ma-ra, Western Thebes, Egypt, c. 1400 BC. It shows Salukis in a procession of spoils of war. This was reproduced from a painting by Dr. Howard Carter that was rendered especially for the Hon. Florence Amherst.

Each of these Salukis was a prize winner at the Saluki and Gazelle Hound Club Show at Ranelagh in 1934. Of special note is the then seldom-seen smooth-coated specimen. This and two others were owned by Miss G. A. Desborough; the rest were owned by the Hon. Florence Amherst.

"The Finding of Moses," a famous painting by Paulo Cagliari Veronese (1528–1588). Veronese was an Italian painter of the Venetian school. He created many detailed masterpieces like the one shown here, in which a page is holding two Salukis (lower left corner).

Reproduction of a 1703 painting by John Wotton, showing a famous Arabian horse, Byerley Turk, and a Saluki of good type. Most of Wotton's paintings of Arabian horses also contained Salukis.

was not until the late 1800s that these dogs really became noticed by Europeans, particularly by the British. The first Salukis probably arrived in England earlier in the 19th century, as evidenced by the famous portrait of the British-bred Saluki named Zilla, painted in 1837, at which time Zilla was kept in the London Zoo. It is a fanciful painting, picturing Zilla with a "handler" in Persian dress.

In 1875, Lady Anne Blunt, married to British diplomat Wilfred Scawen Blunt, made a trip to central Arabia, ending at Basra. She described this adventure in a book, *A Pilgrimage to Nejd*, after traveling from the Mediterranean to the Persian Gulf across Arabia. She acquired two or three Salukis, which she called "greyhounds," from her Bedouin hosts. As to what became of the dogs, nothing is said. These dogs were apparently the smooth-coated desert-bred type. Another extraordinary woman was Gertrude Bell, whose uncle was the British Ambassador to Persia in the 1890s. She was given two feathered Salukis by Fahad Beg ibn Hadhdhal, a sheikh of the Anaizah tribe in Arabia. She called these dogs "Arab greyhounds" and often took them with her when riding. Whether she hunted with them or not is not known.

In 1895, Lady Florence Amherst, the daughter of an Egyptologist, imported the first Salukis into England to have a

Salukis became very popular with the Crusaders. Pictured here is King Henry the Pious of Saxony with a Saluki. Both the king's sleeves and the Saluki's collar are decorated with the pilgrim's badge of a silver scallop shell. Painting by Lucas Cranach (1472–1553), a German painter and etcher.

line of descent surviving to the present. These dogs came from Egypt and were lightly, if at all, feathered, and she termed them "southern strain." She founded the famous Amherstia Kennels and wrote the first published description of the Saluki. This

An ancient picture, representing the grand ceremony in which a white falcon is presented to the great Mughal Emperor Akbar. A Saluki is evident in the foreground.

served as the standard for the breed until 1923, when the Saluki or Gazelle Hound Club was formed and the first English Kennel Club standard for the breed was approved.

In 1919, the National Geographic Society published *The*

Book of Dogs. Listed as the Persian Gazellehound or Slughi, the Saluki is described as a feathered dog, similar to a Greyhound but "short and straight in the body, though very long and rangy of leg. As he stands in profile the outline of fore legs, back, hind legs and ground form an almost perfect square." The article continues to say, "A fact tending to show the antiquity of the Slughi is that no combination of known dogs seems to be capable of producing a creature just like him."

In Hutchinson's *Encyclopedia of Dogs*, the Saluki is described as "graceful, dignified and refined, built on lines that govern speed and endurance. Their limbs are slender with fine quality of bone, and, like the race-horse, they possess subtle strength and power. They are deep chested with plenty of heart room which gives them their wonderful staying power. Elegance in appearance should never be lost sight of, as it indicates the subtle strength peculiar

A modern-day Sloughi, pictured with handler in traditional dress.

Reproduction of a magnificently detailed Veronese painting, depicting the presentation of gifts to the Doge of Venice by Persian ambassadors. Note the Saluki in the foreground.

to desert-bred animals, and is their charm as well as a special gift."

What one must understand is that the Arabic term for all of these dogs simply means "hunting hound." The European phonetic rendition of the Arabic word has been spelled *sloughi, slughi, sleughi, slugi, sloeqi, saluqi* and *saluki*. Some of the confusion arises from the fact that the feathered dogs were more often seen in Iraq and Arabia, whereas the dogs encountered in Egypt, the Sahara and Morocco were more often smooth-coated. In 1935, the French described all of the smooth-coated types as "Sloughi"

and called them a distinct breed. The Kennel Club of England, accepting the 1923 standard, called all of these dogs, feathered or smooth, "Saluqi," in accordance with the Arabic tradition. However, when the standard was published, the spelling was changed to "Saluki." Regional types were recognized by the Arabs by different names. The feathered dogs were called "Slughi Shami" and the smooth dogs were called "Mogrebi Slughi." They also recognized "Akh-taz-eet" (Kirghiz Greyhound) of central Asia and "Tazi," the Saluki of Turkey, Iraq and Iran. Today,

A modern Sloughi, illustrated here, is a recreation of a more ancient smooth-coated dog of northern Africa.

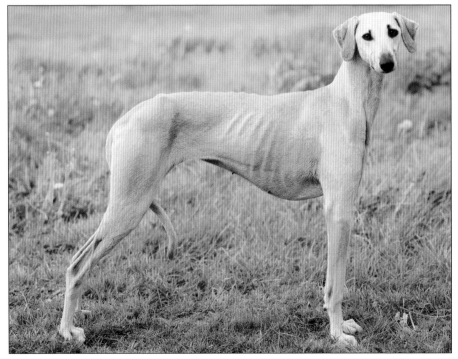

A smooth Saluki allows one to see clearly the distinctive elegance, marked by strength and endurance.

fanciers want to claim that these dogs are different "breeds." The Arabs and their ancestors never considered these dogs as different breeds, just as representatives of different geographic areas. Each breed club today argues vehemently that "their breed" is distinct, based on body measurements, descriptions of gait, height and weight and other such variables. Recent DNA studies indicate that the Saluki and Afghan Hound are the two most ancient of the Saluki Complex.

The modern Sloughi, as recognized by the Fédération Cynologique Internationale (FCI), is a newly created breed. Due to the loss of the nomadic way of life in the French-governed regions of northern Africa in the early part of the 20th century, the hunting hound of the nomads also has all but disappeared. A few apparently pure-bred Sloughis were gathered up and formed the foundation for the Sloughi today. There may have been smooth Salukis and/or Azawakhs registered as Sloughis at this time and earlier. The modern Sloughis are not the same dogs that were described by the early travelers to northern Africa, nor are they the same dogs that were imported into Holland early in the century. Therefore, comparisons of DNA may reflect the cross-breeding that occurred prior to 1971, rather than representing

A Sloughi from northern Africa in the mid-1930s.

the descendants of the original Bedouin or Tuareg dogs.

The Israel Sighthound Club (ISC) was established in 1968. Only two breeds of sighthound were represented in Israel at that time, the Turkuman Afghans and the local Salukis, mostly from Sheikh Suliman El Huzeil's tribe, a prominent group in the Negev Desert. Some also came from Jordan and some from Persia (Iran).

Following the Six Days War in 1967, Saluki lovers in Israel made many trips to the Sinai to visit the Bedouin and to study their dogs. The Sinai Salukis were a bit different from the few Saluki imports to Israel from Europe. They were stronger, somewhat coarser and usually short coated. They had endurance, stamina and very good hunting qualities.

Conversations with European judges who came to Israel to judge dog shows caused the ISC to split

A trio of Kirghiz Greyhounds, or Ahk-taz-eet.

A Barukhzy Hound, also called the Afghan Greyhound, c. 1888.

the breed into Salukis and Sloughis in 1974, thus further compounding the confusion between the Saluki and the Sloughi.

The one good thing that can be said about the Sloughi standard versus the Saluki standard is that the FCI continues to consider the Sloughi to be a "square" dog, whereas the new Saluki standard unfortunately calls for a "rectangular" dog. History and the Arabs support the "square" dog in every case. You cannot change centuries of history by changing the words in a description of the dog. You will only change the subsequent generations, to the detriment of the dog.

SALUKIS IN THE MIDDLE EAST

The Saluki was called "Al-Hurr," the noble one. He was allowed to sleep in the tents, he wore beautiful collars decorated with tiny bells and he was the only dog considered to be "clean." In Islam, all dogs except the Saluki are considered "unclean," and the ordinary dog is called "Kelb." Salukis were never allowed to actually kill game, because Islamic religious practices would not allow the meat to be eaten if this were done. The hounds were used to bring down the game and hold it until the hunter could arrive and ritually dispatch the prey. Hares caught by the hounds were brought back to their masters alive but unconscious. The role of the Saluki as a provider of fresh meat for the pot cannot be overestimated!

The luxuriantly coated Afghan Hound is the Saluki's closest relative based on current DNA analysis.

The Saluki, like the horse, was an integral and indispensable part of the life of the nomadic people of the Middle East. The balance and beauty of both were matters of campfire discussion of no little import! The best animals were often concealed when tribes met. According to tradition, if the visitor admired the animal, it would have to be presented to the guest. Other times, the dogs were given as visible tokens of the trust and honor due the guest. Thus it was that the gene pool of these dogs was widely distributed over a large area, either through "accidental" matings when tribes met or through the dogs' being given as gifts. The European concept of a "breed" was quite foreign to the nomads. They valued their dogs for their ability to hunt and to survive in the harsh environment, not for any imagined specific aspect of the dog.

FOUNDATION OF TODAY'S SALUKI

The Honorable Florence Amherst's first dogs were registered in 1903, two of which she had obtained in 1897 in Egypt. Earlier, in 1900, Miss Lucy Bethell registered a bitch. These three dogs were the first Salukis to leave descendants in the UK. Between 1905 and 1917, Miss Amherst registered almost 60 puppies. During World War I, there were no registrations, but following the war many servicemen returned to England from the Middle East with Salukis. Sarona Kelb, born in Damascus in 1919 and imported by Lt. Col. (later

The Saluki, with thousands of years of selective breeding to make it a fast-running hunting dog, is becoming equally known as a wonderful family pet.

The famous Hon. Florence Amherst, who introduced the Saluki to Britain and wrote the first standards, pictured with litter brothers derived from her imported stock.

General) Lance, was the first Challenge Certificate (award toward a British championship) winner, shown at The Kennel Club show in October 1923. I have always wondered at the use of Kelb in this dog's name, in that the Arabs use the word to mean "unclean." Strange indeed! Another Saluki was also registered in 1919—Hama of Homs, born in Syria and imported by Major C. W. Bayne-Jardine. Over the years leading up to World War II, many other dogs were imported and registered, forming the foundation of the Saluki in Great Britain today. All of these early dogs were clearly "desert-bred," but as more litters were born in England, there was less and less appreciation of the imported dogs.

SALUKIS AND THE AKC
The AKC recognized the Saluki in 1927. The AKC parent club for the breed, the Saluki Club of America, was established in 1924 and still exists today, focused on protecting the breed's best interests.

THE SALUKI IN THE US
The first Saluki known to come to America was a silver-gray brought here by Col. Horace N. Fisher in 1861. The breed was recognized by the American Kennel Club (AKC) in 1927, three years after the founding of the Saluki Club of America

(SCOA) was formed. One of the early serious breeders and exhibitors was Senator Macomber of Rhode Island. Another was Col. Brydon Tennant from Virginia. Their stock was largely from the Sarona kennels of General Lance and the Grevel kennels of Miss Barr in England.

Mrs. Hills (of Redledge in Massachusetts) imported among others several Amherstia Salukis and later helped to start the famous Diamond Hill kennels of Edward K. Aldrich, Jr. in Rhode Island. Mr. Aldrich bred Ch. Marjan II (the first Saluki to win an all-breed Best in Show in America and win the Group at the Westminster Kennel Club show), the foundation dog for Anna Marie Paterno's El Retiro

kennel. Mr. Aldrich also bred Ch. Valda, the foundation dog of Mrs. Esther Knapp's Pine Paddocks kennel. The Diamond Hill line was used by Audrey Hollis Benbow to produce the foundation bitch of Wayne Jensen's Jen Araby kennel on the West Coast. From the latter came the first Saluki of the Srinagar kennel.

In 1945 Mrs. Knapp obtained two desert Salukis from the kennels of King Ibn Saud of Arabia: Ch. Abdul Farouk of Pine Paddocks, a crop-eared male, and Ch. Lady Yeled Sarona Ramullah, a smooth female. The AKC made a special ruling whereby descendants of the pair could be officially registered, even though these dogs were not from an approved registry.

Many famous Salukis are descended from these imports, including Ch. Ahbou Farouk of Pine Paddocks, who was undefeated in the breed. He also received 38 Group Ones and 12 all-breed Bests in Show. Several current lines of American-bred Salukis are founded on these dogs as well.

There are two coat types in Salukis, smooth and feathered. Saluki breeders believe coat type to be a simple dominant-recessive gene, with smooth dominant to feathered. This means if you breed a feathered dog to a feathered dog, you will always get feathered dogs. However, coat types and textures in dogs are not limited to just these two, and it may be that coat type is a more complex polygenetic trait. Certainly, the length of the feathered coat can vary from virtually none to heavily coated dogs, making the dog look almost like an Afghan Hound!

The preference for the feathered Saluki early on in the US resulted in the near loss of smooth Salukis. The formation of the Society for the Perpetuation of Desert Bred Salukis in 1988 and the importation of dogs from the countries of origin helped in re-establishing the smooth Saluki. They are now seen in the show ring quite often and, in fact, a red smooth Saluki won the eastern specialty show in February 2004. She has continued to have a great show career.

SALUKI ANECDOTES

The following stories have been contributed by their author, Dr. John Burchard of Tepe Gawra Salukis:

"Slughis on the Egyptian desert," c. 1930.

A Slughi, bred in England by the Hon. Florence Amherst.

LOST AND FOUND

One of my friends among the Bedouin was an elderly tribesman I shall call Obeid, who at the age of around 90 still took active part in our hunting trips. As a youth, he had a male Saluki whose chief claim to fame was that he could "beat up" all the other Salukis in the tribe, and even the large fierce flock guardian dogs. One fine winter day Obeid set out on a journey to distant hunting grounds, riding his camel, his hooded falcon on his fist and his Saluki trotting alongside. After a while he dozed off with the rhythmic movement of the camel.

The camel stumbled, and Obeid awoke with a start and saw with horror that his falcon, dislodged from its perch by the jolt, was climbing steadily into the sky. This is one of a falconer's worst (and most embarrassing) disasters: when a hooded falcon accidentally becomes airborne, it dares not try to land blindfolded, but will fly straight ahead, climbing all the time, until after many miles it sinks slowly to earth, exhausted, and makes a crash landing. If it cannot then manage to remove the hood, it will soon fall victim to a passing fox or jackal. In any case, it is lost to the falconer. Worse yet, Obeid's Saluki, accustomed to hunting with the falcon, was running off into the distance following the bird, already nearly invisible in the sky.

Thoroughly downcast, Obeid on his camel followed the tracks, hoping at least to recover his hound eventually. After many hours of weary, downhearted progress, Obeid saw a dark speck on the otherwise featureless desert ground. Coming slowly closer, he could make out the form of his Saluki, lying exhausted on the sand. But what was this? The hound held something between his paws. It was the falcon! A hound that attacks falcons is worse than useless to a desert hunter, so with a heavy heart Obeid raised his rifle to shoot the worthless hound. At that moment the falcon stirred, attempting to escape. The hound staggered to his feet, overtook the flapping falcon and again pinned it to the ground.

Like a burst of sunlight came to Obeid the realization that the falcon was unharmed, and his hound was preventing its escape. With joy he gathered up his rumpled but otherwise undamaged falcon, gave water to both hawk and hound, and after a lengthy rest set out on the long homeward journey. Hound and hawk were by then so well recovered that they actually bagged a hare before reaching camp.

KEEPING THE SHEEP

This and the following tale both pertain to a Saluki I knew well in person. His name was La'aban,

ABOVE: A rare Rampur Hound, originating in Rampur in northern India. Some of these dogs were exported to and exhibited in England in the first half of the 20th century. LEFT: A typical modern Saluki of European origin.

and he belonged to a wonderful friend of mine named Barghash An-Naimi. He was directly ancestral to our Tepe Gawra Salukis, and also to those of Elizabeth Dawsari and to those of Mike Ratcliffe in the UK. He was an exceptional hunter and an exceptional personality. His dam Sarha was even more famous, once having caught 12 gazelles in a single day, but that is a different story.

My friend Barghash started life as a Bedouin nomad. As a youth, he took a job with the then new oil company later known as Aramco, and parlayed that into becoming, by the time I knew him, the owner of a prosperous contracting firm.

Myths and legends surround the Saluki even today, as anecdotes abound about the breed's remarkable abilities and feats.

When not traveling or off on a hunting trip—his main preoccupation apart from business—he lived in a large house in Thuqba, a sort of "Arab township" near the bustling town of Al-Khobar on the Saudi Arabian coast opposite Bahrain. Thuqba still allowed "elbow room" for a traditional lifestyle, and so Barghash's household included a flock of sheep, kept at night in the spacious courtyard and taken during the day to graze in the nearby desert—when at least some family members were at home. When nobody was home, the sheep were shut up in the courtyard with an ample supply of hay and water.

Barghash also owned and bred a strikingly beautiful strain of Salukis. The most remarkable hound of this remarkable clan was the aforementioned male named La'aban ("playful one"), whose hunting prowess was celebrated far and wide.

One weekend Barghash went off to spend a few days visiting relatives in Qatar, and the rest of the family went off to visit relatives somewhere else. Someone forgot to close the gate properly and next thing anyone knew, the sheep were wandering the streets of Thuqba. La'aban, also left at home, decided this was not a proper state of affairs, and to the considerable astonishment of the neighbors, proceeded to round up all the sheep and herd them back

Although a hunting hound by nature, the Saluki today also creates a striking presence at dog shows worldwide.

into the courtyard. He then lay down in the open gateway and remained there, preventing the sheep from again leaving the courtyard, for three days, until the master of the house returned.

DUTY CALLS

This story also tells of my friend Barghash and his remarkable and personable Saluki La'aban. La'aban was very much the "boss" of the canine household, especially as he grew older. In typical Arab manner, the Salukis lived in the courtyard, on the cushions of the "majlis," or public sitting room, but were free to come and go as they pleased; the gate was never shut when anyone was at home.

With an eye to an outcross, Barghash acquired a half-grown male Saluki from a different though related line. La'aban hated this upstart newcomer with a passion, and since he wasn't allowed to drive the interloper away, or beat him up, he avoided the pup whenever possible. One fine day, while Barghash and his sons were off doing business in the town, a pickup truck stopped in front of the house. Two young men jumped out, grabbed the puppy, stuffed it in the truck and made a hasty departure. They drove as fast as possible to the large town of Dammam, about 15 miles distant. Somewhere in the maze of side streets, they pulled up in front of a house and disappeared inside, taking the puppy with them.

You'd think La'aban would have heaved a sigh of relief at the sudden disappearance of his hated junior rival, but nothing of the kind. Instead, he set out in hot pursuit of the pickup truck. Of course he was soon outdistanced, but he continued to follow, presumably using his nose (nobody knows for sure) until he found the truck parked in the alley in Dammam. He then jumped into the bed of the pickup and began barking frantically. A crowd soon gathered, drawn by the commotion, and someone recognized La'aban.

A MODERN LOOK AT AN ANCIENT DOG

DNA analysis has given us some new insight into the origin of dogs and the place of the Saluki in the history of the domestic dog. Some studies have used mitochondrial DNA, or mtDNA, analysis. This method involves the analysis of DNA found only in the mitochondria, not the nuclear DNA in the nucleus of the body's cells. During the formation of the embryo, only the mother's cell organelles are inherited through the cytoplasm of the egg. During the entry of the sperm into the egg, all the cell organelles are discarded and only the nuclear DNA is injected. Therefore, the mitochondria can only come from the female parent. Consequently, you can trace ancestors through the maternal, not paternal, line, using mtDNA.

Using this method, you look for the most recent common ancestor of the two individuals. It is assumed that the number of nucleotide (ATCG) variations between two individuals increases with the time of separation from their last common ancestor. In other words, the closer in time the separation is, the higher the number of matching nucleotides.

Mitochondrial DNA evolves very slowly and therefore is useful in examining ancient divisions, those occurring as long ago as 135,000 years ago, but it cannot aid in distinguishing modern "breeds." Most dog breeds have existed for only 400 years or so, and the concept of a closed stud book has existed for only 200 years at best.

Research based on mtDNA conducted in Sweden by Dr. Peter Savolainen indicates that the Saluki has 8 identifiable sequences of mtDNA, 2 of which are unique to the Saluki (sample of 16 dogs). He concludes that there are shared sequences with the Tazi, Akbash Dog, Canaan Dog, Sloughi, Borzoi, Basenji, Afghan Hound and even Tibetan Terrier, those unlikely dogs the Siberian Husky and Alaskan Malamute, and Far Eastern breeds including the Chinese Shar-Pei and Japanese Akita.

Other studies on dog breed relationships are based on microsatellite rather than mtDNA analysis. Microsatellites (also called simple sequence repeats or "nonsense DNA") are repeated sequences where the repeating unit is 1 to 4 nucleotides long. The number of times the unit is repeated in a given microsatellite can be highly variable, a characteristic that makes them useful as genetic markers for rapid changes.

In due course Barghash and his sons, summoned by telephone, arrived on the scene. The young men were identified as owners of the pickup, their house was entered and the puppy was recovered. Barghash didn't say what happened to the young men, but Saudi Arabia does not deal kindly with thieves—and I imagine the neighbors didn't either.

When being used as a marker, the specific number of repetitions in a given microsatellite is not important, but rather the difference in the number of repetitions between sections of the DNA that code for proteins. The variation in the number of repeats affects the overall length of the microsatellite, a characteristic readily measured by laboratory techniques.

A recent study by Parker *et al* (May 21, 2004; *Science*, Vol. 304) is based on such microsatellite data. Using 8 wolves and 85 dog breeds, a sample of 5 individuals of each, they determined that there are 4 basic groups of dogs, the first and earliest group consisting of dogs of Asian and African origins, including the Afghan Hound and the Saluki. It is thought that these dogs are most closely related to the pariah dog type that probably originated in Asia. The common ancestor of the domestic dog is often said to be the gray wolf, *Canis lupus*, based on mtDNA and microsatellite data. A more generalized canid, similar to the smaller canines of Asia and possibly Africa, is hypothesized as a more likely common ancestor by several researchers. This latter conclusion is based on behavior, morphology and genetic data.

Assuming the wolf as the ancestor of the domestic dog, the first division, according to Parker, is between the Far Eastern breeds such as the Shar-Pei and Chow Chow and all other breeds. The second division occurs between the Basenji and the remaining breeds. The third division occurs between the Northern breeds such as the Husky and Eskimo Dog and all other breeds. Then the Saluki and Afghan Hound are split away from all other breeds.

Based on these data, several breeds thought to be closely related to the Saluki were found to be quite modern, including the Greyhound, Pharaoh Hound and Ibizan Hound. The Tazi, Akbash Dog, Azawakh and Sloughi were not included in Parker's study.

The fact that there are so many relationships with such diverse breeds indicates the ancient origin of the Saluki, an amalgam of the Middle East and Far East. This information also indicates that the Saluki is a unique breed separate from the other dogs often considered the Saluki Complex. It is hoped that further research on DNA will help us understand the relationships of these breeds more clearly. Thus, one must conclude that the Saluki is an ancient combination of several maternal lines, forming a breed over time.

The Saluki is prized for his aristocratic air as well as his sense of duty and intelligence.

CHARACTERISTICS OF THE
SALUKI

SALUKI TRAINABILITY

The most common statement one encounters about the Saluki is that he is "reserved," "standoff-ish" and "difficult." Sighthounds in general, and Salukis in particular, have their own opinions about what is acceptable and what is not. While loving and warm with their families, enjoying attention and affection from members of their "pack," they are very wary of strangers.

Salukis also have very clear ideas about what they will and will not do! Trying to convince a Saluki that the food you have so carefully prepared is exactly what he should be eating, when he clearly has determined it is not, can be trying, at best, and very frustrating.

Many people think you cannot train a Saluki at all. Here I have to disagree. You can train a Saluki as well as any other hound, but you need a great deal of patience. You need to give the dog time to process the command and finally decide to respond. A Saluki will never respond the way

The Saluki is not the dog for everyone. Training a Saluki requires patience, knowledge, determination and often a bit of convincing on the trainer's part. Do you have what it takes to own and train a Saluki?

a retriever does! Salukis were not bred to honor the whims of man; rather, it's the other way around. There is nothing worse than an undisciplined dog, and Salukis are no exception. The training technique has to be tailored to fit the individual, but they can be taught anything that any other dog can do. Patience is the key word. You will never force a Saluki to do anything. Instead, you must convince the dog that it was his idea, not yours. This type of training requires a very dog-knowledgeable person, and one with infinite patience.

"Come," like other commands, is honored by the Saluki when he

gets around to it! Nevertheless, training the pup early on is critical in getting him to come when called. The independent nature of the dog combined with the intelligence of this breed can make this a battle of wills. If you let the dog win once, you have lost forever. The Saluki memory is long! When working with one of these dogs, recognizing the inherent good sense that the breed possesses as well as its independent nature is crucial to your success.

There is no reason why a Saluki cannot be crate-trained, as are other hounds. Some in the dog world think that Salukis "need to be free" to express their desert nature, but in today's world, this is a recipe for disaster. However, a Saluki does not need to be on lead at all times either. Once you have taught the dog to come when called, he will, but in his own time. Treats, commonly used in training many breeds, are not especially useful here. Salukis

This young man went to "crate" lengths to coax his Saluki to come on in!

HEART-HEALTHY

In this modern age of ever-improving cardio-care, no doctor or scientist can dispute the advantages of owning a dog to lower a person's risk of heart disease. Studies have proven that petting a dog, walking a dog and grooming a dog all show positive results toward lowering your blood pressure. The simple routine of exercising your dog—going outside with the dog and walking, jogging or playing catch—is heart-healthy in and of itself. If you are normally less active than your physician thinks you should be, adopting a dog may be a smart option to improve your own quality of life as well as that of another creature.

sometimes are interested in food, but often not. You must develop a working relationship with your dog that is based on mutual respect. Once you have this partnership established, your Saluki will do anything you ask, provided you give him leeway to accomplish the task at his pace.

PACK MENTALITY

Another characteristic of the coursing hounds is their ability and desire to work in groups. Two or three hounds coursing prey is the most wonderful sight any enthusiast could hope for! The teamwork and communication that goes on between these dogs as they overtake and bring down game is a marvel to watch. The pack instinct in these dogs is very strong, and that is one reason that they are such wonderful family dogs.

There is usually a pack leader, the "Alpha" dog, to whom all other dogs in the pack look for direction. The "Alpha" dog idea has been greatly overblown, as the role may switch from dog to dog under changed circumstances. In most packs, it is the eldest female. Before one even thinks about acquiring a Saluki, one must understand the "pack leader" role and be willing to assume it. Dogs, like children, prefer direction and a set of consistent rules by which to live. If you are considering a Saluki, you should read every-

DELTA SOCIETY
The human-animal bond propels the work of the Delta Society, striving to improve the lives of people and animals. The Pet Partners Program proves that the lives of people and dogs are inextricably linked. The Pet Partners Program, a national registry, trains and screens volunteers for pet therapy in hospices, nursing homes, schools and rehabilitation centers. Dog-and-handler teams of Pet Partners volunteer in all 50 states, with nearly 7,000 teams making visits annually. About 900,000 patients, residents and students receive assistance each year. If you and your dog are interested in becoming Pet Partners, contact the Delta Society online at www.deltasociety.org.

A Saluki in full flight is the picture of exuberance and athletic grace.

Agility training allows a Saluki to use both his brain and his athleticism. It is a sport that the breed enjoys and to which it is well suited.

thing you can find about canine behavior and the role of the pack leader. If you attempt to bring one of these dogs into your home without understanding these things, your life will be one of misery and the dog will undoubtedly be returned to the breeder! Most conscientious breeders will explain all of this to you in great detail prior to your purchase of the Saluki puppy. There are many resources available to you in bookstores and on the Internet; do not neglect to inform yourself! These dogs are not for everyone, by any criterion, and more so than with other breeds, you need to do your homework.

HEALTH AND SPECIAL TRAITS

Salukis are very clean dogs around the house. They keep both themselves and their surroundings immaculate. House-training is very simple with these dogs, as they do not want to foul their sleeping areas. They are also very healthy dogs, with few, if any, of the problems commonly associated with small gene pools. Hip dysplasia is unknown, and thyroid problems are minimal.

The Saluki Club of America has recently reported an increase in the number of cases of cancers related to the heart (cardiac hemangiosarcoma). Various defects in the heart valves were also reported. When selecting a breeder, this is an important consideration, as this is a fatal condition. Sudden death was the most common identifying factor.

Also consider this sighthound's sight. Glaucoma and progressive retinal atrophy (PRA) have been identified as potential problems. Given the overall health problems common to so many pure-bred dogs, the Saluki is a remarkably healthy breed and the overall incidence of these problems is relatively small.

The only real drawback to this breed and its relatives is possible temperament problems. If these dogs are not properly socialized at a very early age, they can be very fearful, snap at both people and dogs and show other aspects of fear-biting. One must realize that the Saluki, in his traditional environment, grows up as a dog that fends for himself, is surrounded by a large extended family, both canine and human, and lives among many other domesticated animals. If a dog is isolated from both canine and human companions in his formative stages (seven to twelve weeks of age), much of the damage has already been done and cannot be corrected.

Taking your new pup out to visit friends and neighbors,

human and canine, is the most important thing you can do. Many, if not most, veterinarians advise against taking the pup out until he is fully inoculated. For Salukis, this delay is guaranteed to create temperament problems. One must balance the risk of infection (*slight*) against long-term temperament problems (*great*) by not socializing the pup early on.

These elegant, intelligent and self-sufficient dogs are a joy to own, but both you and the dog must have the correct temperament. A Saluki will be your loyal companion, friend and elegant housemate, as long as you respect the heritage and history of this ancient breed. Their beauty is unsurpassed, and once you come to know and understand them their intelligence will leave you breathless. This is a special breed for special people.

This is an example of the double suspension gallop epitomized by the Saluki. Compare this photo to the facing page and you will see that, at both extremes, the dog's feet do not touch the ground.

BREED STANDARD FOR THE

SALUKI

The breed standard for the Saluki is a matter of great controversy at the moment. The original description written by Lady Florence Amherst in 1907 was used as the standard for many years. In 1923 the Saluki or Gazelle Hound Club was formed in Britain and an official standard, slightly revised from Lady Amherst's description, was adopted by The Kennel Club of England. Recently both The Kennel Club and the Fédération Cynologique Internationale (FCI) adopted new standards that have met with great resistance from a number of Saluki fanciers. The primary objection lies in the addition of a new section, "Important Proportions" that is not included in the 1998 UK standard but is in the 1997 FCI standard. This states that the dog should appear as a "slightly elongated rectangle" which is contrary to all previous standards, as well as contrary to the majority of dogs that exist today.

Many terms used in dog standards were based on the understanding of horse anatomy from the Victorian era. These terms are not appropriate for dogs, nor were many even used correctly with respect to horses. A prime example is the phrase "hocks well let down." This is often interpreted to mean that the heel should be close to the ground. In fact, what this means is that the length of the calcaneal process, the "heel bone," should be relatively short and does not refer to the length of the metatarsi, the bones from the heel to the ground. In order to have the spring for sprint speed and for jumping, a relatively longer distance between ground and heel gives the dog a decided advantage, especially when combined with length in the humerus and femur. This combination gives the dog speed, endurance and jumping power. Examples of long or "high" hocks are the cat and the rabbit. They possess great initial speed, good jumping and climbing (or digging) power, but no endurance. In Lady Amherst's original description of the Saluki, she used the phrase "hocks well let down, showing plenty of galloping and jumping power." This gives one a better sense of what is meant than the current wording. One does not want the point of the hock (equivalent to a human heel) to be close to the ground, but rather that the actual bone process should be shorter instead of longer. There must be a balance between the height from the ground and the length of the calcaneal process to achieve the desired speed, agility and endurance of the Saluki.

The Saluki is a breed of great antiquity and has been bred in its native lands for thousands of years as a functional hunting hound. It would seem that changing a standard to fit the current crop of show dogs is clearly a setback for those who are trying to preserve the breed as it was originally developed. We know that the dog is a very plastic animal. Humans can mold this creature into any form we desire, by selectively choosing those dogs with the appropriate characteristics. New "breeds" appear all the time and some actually gain recognition. As the Saluki has one of the oldest documented histories of all breeds, perhaps one should rely on history and function rather than current fleets of "the fancy."

While reading on, this may seem very tedious to the newcomer! However, by examining the differences in the standards, from the original to today, and from country to country, one may gain a better perspective of

FOR THE LOVE OF DOGS

Breeding involves a major financial investment, but just as important is your investment in time. You'll spend countless hours in caring for, cleaning (and cleaning up after), feeding and training the litter. Furthermore, we haven't yet mentioned the strain and health risks that delivering a litter pose to the dam. Many bitches die in puppybirth, and that is a very high price to pay. Experienced breeders, with established lines and reputations in the field, are not in the hobby for financial gain. Those "breeders" who are in it for profit are not true breeders at all, and are not reputable sources from which to buy puppies. Remember, there is nothing more to breeding dogs than the love of the dogs and the breed.

this breed. Following is the original standard, compared with the pre-1997 British, current Kennel Club, American Kennel Club (AKC), Canadian Kennel Club (CKC) and FCI standards. It is hoped that this information will give the prospective Saluki owner a better view of the design and purpose of this marvelous sighthound than any one standard by itself. You may also begin to appreciate the difficulty of describing a living, vibrant animal in mere words.

COMPARISON OF THE BREED STANDARDS

BRIEF HISTORICAL SUMMARY:
Current (2000) FCI Standard:
Salukis vary in type and the variation is desired and typical for the breed. The reason for the variation is the special place held by the Saluki in the Arab tradition and the immense size of the Middle East area where the Saluki has

been used as a hound of the chase for thousands of years. Originally each tribe had Salukis best suited for hunting the particular game in its own area, but by Middle East tradition, Salukis are not bought or sold but presented as marks of honour. It follows that those presented as such to Europeans and brought to Europe came from a wide variation of terrain and climate and vary accordingly. The British 1923 standard was the first official European breed standard for the Saluki and was drawn up to cover all these original types of Saluki.

GENERAL APPEARANCE
How the Arabs judged Salukis
(From *Hutchinson's Dog Encyclopedia*): The main slope of the body should be from tail to shoulder, giving an impression of speed, the hindquarters being higher than the shoulders. An arched back with spine showing is considered a sign of speed.

Faulty head, exhibiting snipy foreface, cheeky, apple-headed with rounded topskull.

Correct head.

Faulty head, coarse with Roman nose.

Undesirable profile, showing straight shoulders and ewe neck; poor topline, dipping behind shoulders and high in rear; tailset too high with kinked tail; lacking angulation in rear.

Correct profile.

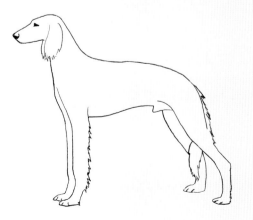

Undesirable profile, showing poor topline, dropping off in rear like a Whippet; over-angulated rear; flat feet; weak sloping pasterns.

Original (1923) UK Standard: The whole appearance of this breed should give an impression of grace and symmetry and of great speed and endurance coupled with strength and activity to enable it to kill gazelle or other quarry over deep sand or rocky mountain. The expression should be dignified and gentle, with deep, faithful, far-seeing eyes. The Smooth Variety. In this variety the points should be the same with the exception of the coat, which has no feathering.

Current (2000) UK Standard: Gives impression of grace, symmetry and of great speed and endurance, coupled with strength and activity.

Pre-1997 UK, current (1999) CKC Standards: Identical to the original, except the smooth variety is described elsewhere in the standards.

Current FCI Standard: The whole appearance of this breed should give an impression of grace and symmetry and of great speed and endurance coupled with strength and activity. Smooth variety: the points should be the same with the exception of the coat which has no feathering. Important Proportions: The length of the body (from point of shoulder to point of buttock) is approximately equal to the height at the withers, although the dog often gives the impression of being longer than he really is.

AKC Standard: The whole appearance of this breed should give an impression of grace and symmetry and of great speed and endurance coupled with strength and activity to enable it to kill gazelle or other quarry over deep sand or rocky mountain. The expression should be dignified and gentle, with deep, faithful, far-seeing eyes.

CHARACTERISTICS/TEMPERAMENT
Original, Pre-1997 UK, AKC and CKC Standards: Not detailed.

Current UK (2000) Standard: Characteristics: Great variation in type due to wide geographical area of origin. There are both feathered and smooth varieties. The expression should be dignified and gentle with faithful, far-seeing eyes. Light flowing movement. Temperament: Reserved with strangers but not nervous or aggressive. Dignified, intelligent and independent.

Current FCI Standard: Behavior/Temperament: Reserved with strangers, but not nervous or aggressive. Dignified, intelligent and independent.

HEAD AND SKULL
Arab Judging: There should be

two fingers' width across the top of the head between the ears. There should be plenty of loose skin in the cheek.

Original Standard: Long and narrow, skull moderately wide between the ears, not domed, stop not pronounced, the whole showing great quality. Nose black or liver.

Pre-1997 UK, current UK, AKC, and CKC Standards: Identical.

Current FCI Standard: Head: Long and narrow, the whole showing nobility. Cranial Region: Moderately wide between ears, not domed. Stop: Not pronounced. Facial Region: Nose: Black or liver brown.

EYES
Original Standard: Dark to hazel and bright, large and oval, but not prominent.

Pre-1997 UK, current UK, AKC and CKC Standards: Identical.

Current FCI Standard: Dark to hazel and bright, large and oval, but not prominent. The expression should be dignified and gentle with faithful and far-seeing eyes.

EARS
Arab Judging: Ears should be long and finely feathered.

The various standards agree that the head should be long and narrow, without a pronounced stop.

Original Standard: Long and covered with long silky hair hanging close to the skull, and mobile.

Pre-1997 UK and CKC Standards: Long and mobile, covered with long silky hair; hanging close to the skull.

Current UK Standard: Long and mobile, not too low set, covered with long silky hair, hanging close to skull. Bottom tip of leather reaches to corner of mouth when brought forward. Provided ear is covered with silky hair which may grow only from top half, the standard is complied with but longer hair also correct.

Current FCI Standard: Long and covered with long silky hair, set on high, mobile, hanging close to the skull.

AKC Standard: Long and covered with long silky hair hanging close to the skull and mobile.

MOUTH
Original Standard: Teeth: Strong and level.

Pre-1997 UK and CKC Standards: Teeth strong and level.

Current UK Standard: Teeth and jaws strong with a perfect, rectangular and complete scissor bite, i.e., upper teeth closely overlapping lower teeth and set square to the jaws.

Current FCI Standard: Teeth and jaws are strong with a perfect, regular and complete scissor bite.

AKC Standard: Teeth strong and level.

NECK
Original Standard: Long, supple and well muscled.

All Other Standards: Identical.

FOREQUARTERS
Arab Judging: Forelegs: Elbows should be difficult to press together. Wrists should be small, and paws point forward at a small angle. The first thing the Arab always looks at is the chest: this must be deep and strong.

Original Standard: Shoulders sloping and set well back, well muscled without being coarse. Chest: Deep and moderately narrow. Forelegs: Straight and long from the elbow to the knee.

Pre-1997 UK and CKC Standards: Shoulders sloping and set well back, well muscled without being coarse. The chest deep and moderately narrow. The forelegs straight and long from the elbow to the knee.

Current UK Standard: Shoulders sloping and set well back, well muscled without being coarse. Chest deep and moderately narrow, when viewed from front not an inverted V. Forelegs straight and long from elbow to wrist. Pasterns strong and slightly sloping. Not round boned. Humerus sloping slightly backwards.

Current FCI Standard: Shoulders: Well laid back, well muscled without being coarse. Upper arm: Approximately equal in length to the shoulder blade and forming a good angle with it. Forearm: Long and straight from elbow to wrist. Pasterns: Strong and flexible, slightly sloping.

AKC Standard: Shoulders sloping and set well back, well muscled without being coarse. Forelegs: The forelegs straight and long from the elbow to the knee.

BODY
Arab Judging: An arched back with spine showing is considered a sign of speed.

Original Standard: Loin and Back: Back fairly broad, muscles slightly arched over the loin.

Current FCI Standard: Back: Fairly broad. Loin: Slightly arched and well muscled. Croup: Hipbones set wide apart. Chest: Deep, long and moderately narrow. Neither barrel ribbed nor slab sided. Underline: Well tucked up.

Pre-1997 UK and CKC Standard: Back fairly broad, muscles slightly arched over the loin.

Current UK Standard: Identical, then adds "but never roach backed. Brisket long and deep, not barrel-ribbed or slab-sided, with good cut-up. Sufficient length of loin important."

AKC Standard: Back fairly broad, muscles slightly arched over the loin.

HINDQUARTERS
Arab Judging: Loins should be very narrow. There should be a width of three or four fingers between the two hip bones on the top of the back; a deep hollow between these bones is thought very good. Back Legs: Hock must be very pronounced and the lower the better.

Original Standard: Strong, hip bones set wide apart, and the stifle moderately bent, hocks low to the ground, showing galloping and jumping power. *NOTE:* A comma follows the first word.

Pre-1997 UK, AKC and CKC Standards: Identical.

Current UK Standard: Strong hip bones set wide apart. Stifle moderately bent with well developed first and second thigh. Hocks low to ground.

Current FCI Standard: Strong, showing galloping and jumping power. Upper and lower thighs: Well developed. Stifle: Moderately bent. Hocks: Well let down.

FEET
Arab Judging: Rear paws: There should be a pronounced flatness here showing easy quick turning at speed.

Original Standard: Of moderate length, toes long, and well arched, not splayed out, but at the same time not cat-footed; the whole being strong and supple and well feathered between the toes.

Pre-1997 UK, AKC and CKC Standard: Identical.

Current UK Standard: Strong, supple, of moderate length, toes long and well arched, not splayed out, but at the same time not cat footed. Feathered between the toes (except the smooth variety). Front feet may point outwards at a very slight angle when standing.

Current FCI Standard: Front feet: Feet of moderate length, toes long and well arched, not splayed, but at the same time not cat-footed; the whole being strong and supple; feathered between the toes. Hind feet: Similar to front feet.

TAIL
Arab Judging: Feathering must be fine and regular. The tail when pulled down between the legs and round up the back should reach to the point between the hip bones.

Original, Pre-1997 UK and CKC Standards: Long, set on low and carried naturally in a curve, well feathered on the underside with long silky hair, not bushy.

Current UK Standard: Set on low from long and gently sloping pelvis. Carried naturally in a curve. Well feathered on underside but not bushy. In adults not carried above line of back except in play. Tip reaching to hock.

Current FCI Standard: Long, set on low and carried naturally in a curve, well feathered on the underside with long silky hair, not bushy. In adults not carried above the topline except in play. Tip reaching at least to the point of hock.

AKC Standard: Long, set on low and carried naturally in a curve, well feathered on the underside with long silky hair, not bushy.

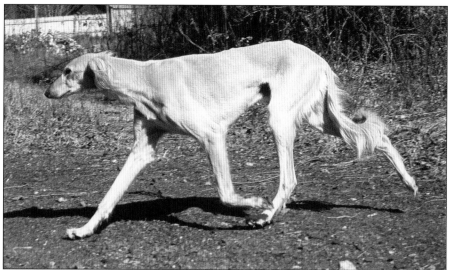

The Saluki gait should appear fluid and effortless, with reach and drive that allows the dog to cover much ground.

GAIT/MOVEMENT
Original, Pre-1997 UK, AKC and CKC Standards: Not detailed.

Current UK Standard: Smooth, flowing and effortless. Light and lifting, showing both reach and drive without hackney action or pounding.

Current FCI Standard: Smooth, flowing and effortless at trot. Light and lifting showing both reach and drive without hackney action or pounding.

COAT
Original Standard: Smooth and of a soft silky texture, slight feather on the legs, feather at the back of the thighs, and sometimes with slight woolly feather on thigh and shoulders.

Pre-1997 UK and CKC Standards: Smooth and of a soft silky texture; slight feather on the legs; feather at the back of the thighs; sometimes with slight woolly feather on thigh and shoulders. (In the smooth variety the points should

A well-marked young Saluki with black and tan coloration, revealing his fascination for breed standards!

be the same with the exception of the coat which has no feathering.)

Current UK Standard: Smooth and of soft silky texture, feathering on legs and back of thighs, puppies may have slight woolly feathering on thighs and shoulder. Feathering may occur on throat. In the smooth variety the coat is the same but without feathering.

Current FCI Standard: Hair: Smooth and of a soft, silky texture, feathering on the legs and at the back of thighs, feathering may be present on the throat in adults, puppies may have slight woolly feather on thighs and shoulders. The smooth variety has no feathering.

AKC Standard: Smooth and of a soft silky texture; slight feather on the legs; feather at the back of the thighs; sometimes with slight woolly feather on thigh and shoulders.

Color
Original Standard: White, cream, fawn, golden, red, grizzle and tan, tricolour (white, black and tan) and black and tan.

Pre-1997 UK Standard: White, cream, fawn, golden, red, grizzle and tan, tricolour (white, black and tan) and black and tan, or variations of these colors.

Current UK Standard: Any colour or combination of colours permissible, other than brindle.

CKC Standard: White, cream, fawn, golden, red, grizzle, and tan, tricolour (white, black and tan), black and tan, or any of the aforementioned colours and white.

Current FCI Standard: Any colour or combination of colours is permissible. Brindles are undesirable.

AKC Standard: White cream, fawn, golden, red, grizzle and tan, tricolor (white, black and tan) and black and tan.

Size
Original Standard: Dogs should average in height from 23 to 28 inches, and the bitches may be considerably smaller, this being very typical of the breed.

Pre-1997 UK Standard: Height should average 58–71 cm (23–28 ins). Bitches proportionately smaller.

Current UK and FCI Standards: Dogs: 58–71 cm (23–28 ins) at shoulders; Bitches: proportionately smaller.

AKC and CKC Standards: Dogs should average in height from 23–28 inches and bitches may be

MEETING THE IDEAL
The American Kennel Club defines a standard as: "A description of the ideal dog of each recognized breed, to serve as an ideal against which dogs are judged at shows." This "blueprint" is drawn up by the breed's recognized parent club, approved by a majority of its membership, and then submitted to the AKC for approval. The AKC states that "An understanding of any breed must begin with its standard. This applies to all dogs, not just those intended for showing." The picture that the standard draws of the dog's type, gait, temperament and structure is the guiding image used by breeders as they plan their programs.

considerably smaller, this being very typical of this breed.

SMOOTH VARIETY
All Other Standards: No distinctions are made.

AKC Standard: In this variety the points should be the same with the exception of the coat, which has no feathering.

FAULTS
Original, AKC and CKC Standards: Not detailed.

Pre-1997 UK and FCI Standards: Any departure from the foregoing points should be considered a fault and the seriousness with which the fault should be regarded should be in exact proportion to its degree.

Current UK: Identical, then adds "and its effect upon the health and welfare of the dog."

NOTE: It is assumed, of course, that male dogs will have two normally descended testicles, although the only standards to specify this are the current UK and FCI standards.

AUTHOR'S SUMMARY
From this discussion, I hope the reader can see that the standard has only recently been changed, and probably not for the better. The Saluki is a hunting breed, used for thousands of years in every terrain imaginable. To attempt to define the "show gait" or the "proportion" of the dog after all these years seems not only unnecessary but superfluous. I leave it to the prospective buyer to seek out the type of Saluki he most desires, armed with these comparisons. In that way, everyone should be able to find the dog that most conforms to the mind's eye. I am sure this controversy will continue for many years. There is no one perfect Saluki, nor one perfect standard.

SALUKI

WHERE TO BEGIN?

If you are convinced that the Saluki is the ideal dog for you, it's time to learn about where to find a puppy and what to look for. Locating a litter of Salukis should not present a problem for the new owner. You should inquire about breeders in your area who enjoy a good reputation in the breed. You are looking for an established breeder with outstanding dog

Have a selection of interesting and safe toys ready for your Saluki pup's arrival to your home.

ethics and a strong commitment to the breed. New owners should have as many questions as they have doubts. An established breeder is indeed the one to answer your four million questions and make you comfortable with your choice of the Saluki. An established breeder will sell you a puppy at a fair price if, and only if, the breeder determines that you are a suitable, worthy owner of his/her dogs. An established breeder can be relied upon for advice, at any reasonable time of day. A reputable breeder will accept a puppy back, without questions, should you decide that this not the right dog for you.

When choosing a breeder, reputation is much more important than convenience of location. Do not be overly impressed by breeders who run brag advertisements about their stupendous champions and working lines. The real quality breeders are quiet and unassuming. You hear about them at performance trials and shows, by word of mouth. You may be well advised to avoid the novice who lives only a couple of miles away. The local novice breeder, trying so hard to get rid

Grooming is but one of the responsibilities to which you must be ready to commit, from puppyhood throughout your Saluki's life.

FINDING A QUALIFIED BREEDER

Before you begin your puppy search, ask for references from your vet, other breeders and other Saluki owners to refer you to someone they believe is reputable. Responsible breeders usually raise only one or two breeds of dog. Avoid any breeder who has several different breeds or has several litters at the same time. Dedicated breeders are usually involved with a breed or other dog club. Many participate in some sport or activity related to their breed. Just as you want to be assured of the breeder's qualifications, the breeder wants to be assured that you will make a worthy owner. Expect the breeder to interview you, asking questions about your goals for the pup, your experience with dogs and what kind of home you will provide.

of that first litter of puppies, is more than accommodating and anxious to sell you one. That breeder will charge you as much as any established breeder. The novice breeder isn't going to interrogate you and your family about your intentions with the puppy, the environment and training you can provide, etc. That breeder will be nowhere to be found when your poorly bred, badly adjusted four-pawed monster starts to growl, pick a fight with the cat and generally wreak havoc. Similarly, the impulse purchase of a cute Saluki pup with an unknown background will not provide the support, education and guidance you will need.

The Saluki pup will settle into his new home and feel confident and at ease.

While health considerations in the Saluki are not nearly as daunting as in most other breeds, socialization is a breeder concern of immense importance. Since the Saluki's temperament can vary from line to line, socialization is the first and best way to encourage a proper, stable personality.

Choosing a breeder is an important first step in dog ownership. Fortunately, the majority of Saluki breeders are devoted to the breed and its well-being. New owners should have little problem finding a reputable breeder who doesn't live on the other side of the country (or in a different country). The American Kennel Club and Saluki Club of America are trusted sources for breeder referrals. Potential owners are encouraged to attend shows and racing and coursing trials to see the Salukis in action, to meet the owners and handlers firsthand and to get an idea what Salukis

look like outside a photographer's lens. Provided you approach the handlers when they are not busy with the dogs, most are more than willing to answer questions, recommend breeders and give advice.

Now that you have contacted and met a breeder or two and made your choice about which breeder is best suited to your needs, it's time to visit the litter. Keep in mind that many top breeders have waiting lists. Sometimes new owners have to wait a year or longer for a puppy. If you are really committed to the breeder whom you've selected, then you will wait (and hope for an early arrival!). If not, you may have to go with to your second- or third-choice breeder. Don't be too anxious, however. If the breeder doesn't have any waiting list, or any customers, there is probably a

GETTING ACQUAINTED

When visiting a litter, ask the breeder for suggestions on how best to interact with the puppies. If possible, get right into the middle of the pack and sit down with them. Observe which pups climb into your lap and which ones shy away. Toss a toy for them to chase and bring back to you. It's easy to fall in love with the puppy who picks you, but keep your future objectives in mind before you make your final decision.

good reason. It's no different from visiting a restaurant with no clientele. The better establishments always have waiting lists—and it's usually worth the wait. Besides, isn't a puppy more important than a nice meal?

Since you are likely choosing a Saluki as a pet dog and not a working dog, you simply should select a pup that is friendly and attractive. Salukis generally have large litters, averaging eight puppies, so selection can be overwhelming once you have located a desirable litter. Without proper socialization, temperament may present trouble in certain strains. Beware of the shy or overly aggressive puppy; be especially conscious of the nervous Saluki pup. Don't let sentiment or emotion trap you into buying the runt of the litter, if such exists.

If you have intentions of your new charge racing or coursing, there are many more considerations. The parents of a future working or performance dog should have excellent qualifications, including actual field experience as well as working titles in their pedigrees.

The sex of your puppy is largely a matter of personal taste, although there is a common belief among those who work with Salukis that bitches are quicker to learn and generally more loving and faithful. Males learn more slowly but retain the lesson longer.

The difference in size is quite noticeable, with males being considerably larger. Coloration is not a grave concern with this breed, although there have been countless treatises on the actual colors available in Saluki. Breeders cannot seem to agree even to identify the color of an individual in front of them. Some will call a dog "deer-grizzle," while another might

SELECTING FROM THE LITTER

Before you visit a litter of puppies, promise yourself that you won't fall for the first pretty face you see! Decide on your goals for your puppy—show prospect, field dog, obedience competitor, family companion—and then look for a puppy who displays the appropriate qualities. In most litters, there is an Alpha pup (the bossy puppy), and occasionally a shy fellow who is less confident, with the rest of the litter falling somewhere in the middle. "Middle-of-the-roaders" are safe bets for most families and novice competitors.

call the same dog a "gray-grizzle." There is a huge discrepancy between golden, red and golden red. Nevertheless, a good stable dog, with working abilities, can be any color, and owners should curb their preconceived notions about the color of their Saluki.

Always check the bite of your selected puppy to be sure that it is neither overshot nor undershot. While incorrect bites are rare, it is important to check. Sometimes a dog may have a faulty jaw when young, but the problem corrects itself with maturity. The lower jaw is the last bone of the body to grow, so patience is often rewarded. If the pup was born with an incorrect bite, it will normally be correct by about the age of two. However, when a pup is born with an overbite or under-bite, or a wry mouth, it will not correct.

Color is a matter of personal preference, and the Saluki offers an array of possibilities. Foremost concerns, though, should be good health and sound temperament.

PEDIGREE VS. REGISTRATION CERTIFICATE

Too often new owners are confused between these two important documents. Your puppy's pedigree, essentially a family tree, is a written record of a dog's genealogy of three generations or more. The pedigree will show you the names as well as performance titles of all dogs in your pup's background. Your breeder must provide you with a registration application, with his part properly filled out. You must complete the application and send it to the AKC with the proper fee. Every puppy must come from a litter that has been AKC-registered by the breeder, born in the US and from a sire and dam that are also registered with the AKC.

The seller must provide you with complete records to identify the puppy. The AKC requires that the seller provide the buyer with the following: breed; sex, color and markings; date of birth; litter number (when available); names and registration numbers of the parents; breeder's name; and date sold or delivered.

Fortunately, commercial breeders are rarely attracted to the breed. This also helps your selection, ensuring that most pups will come from proven lines unencumbered by overbreeding, inbreeding or the countless finicky prejudices that have damaged other breeds.

Prices vary from country to country and from breeder to breeder. Any reputable Saluki breeder, if assured of a good home and one where the dog will actually be out in the field, will likely make a number of concessions regarding price. It is entirely up to the breeder and the prospective buyer to negotiate the terms and conditions under which the pup will be sold. The primary concern for everyone is to be sure the dog is placed in a stable home where he will receive the necessary care and exercise. Salukis are not for the faint of heart, nor are they comfortable in confined settings.

Breeders commonly allow visitors to see the litter by around the fifth or sixth week, and puppies leave for their new homes between the eighth and tenth week. Breeders who permit their

Curious Saluki puppies like to evaluate the potential owners, too!

puppies to leave early are more interested in your money than their puppies' well-being. Puppies need to learn the rules of the trade from their dam, and most dams continue teaching the pups manners and dos and don'ts until around the eighth week. Breeders spend significant amounts of time with the Saluki toddlers so that they are able to interact with the "other species," i.e., humans. Given the long history that dogs and humans have, bonding between the two species is natural but must be nurtured. A well-bred, well-socialized Saluki pup wants nothing more than to be near you and please you, even though at times it appears that he has no interest in you and yours. Salukis are born to be independent, but they are truly devoted to their families. Despite their very strong streak of independence, they would be lost without you. Proper training, using only positive reinforcement, is the key to success with a Saluki.

THE FAMILY TREE

Your puppy's pedigree is his family tree. Just as a child may resemble his parents and grandparents, so too will a puppy reflect the qualities, good and bad, of his ancestors, especially those in the first two generations. Therefore it's important to know as much as possible about a puppy's immediate relatives. Reputable and experienced breeders should be able to explain the pedigree and why they chose to breed from the particular dogs they used.

research, breeder selection and puppy visitation are very important aspects of finding the puppy of your dreams. Beyond that, these things also lay the foundation for a successful future with your pup. We've mentioned how puppy personalities within each litter vary. By spending time with the puppies, you will be able to recognize certain behaviors and what these behaviors indicate about each pup's temperament. Which type of pup will complement your family dynamics is best determined by observing the puppies in action within their "pack." Your breeder's expertise and recommendations are also very valuable. Although you may fall in love with a bold and brassy male, the

The acquisition of a Saluki should be a family affair, since the entire family will have to cooperate in the dog's care and training.

A COMMITTED NEW OWNER

By now you should understand what makes the Saluki a most unique and special dog, one that you feel will fit nicely into your family and lifestyle. If you have researched breeders, you should be able to recognize a knowledgeable and responsible Saluki breeder who cares not only about his pups but also about what kind of owner you will be. If you have completed the final step in your new journey, you have found a litter, or possibly two, of quality Saluki pups.

A visit with the puppies and their breeder should be an education in itself. You see how breed

breeder may suggest that another pup would be best for you. The breeder's experience in rearing Saluki pups and matching their temperaments with appropriate humans offers the best assurance that your pup will meet your needs and expectations. The type of puppy that you select is just as important as your decision that the Saluki is the breed for you.

The decision to live with a Saluki is a serious commitment and not one to be taken lightly. This puppy is a living sentient being that will be dependent on you for basic survival for his entire life. Beyond the basics of survival—food, water, shelter and protection—he needs much, much more. The new pup needs love,

Showing off for the visitors! Be sure to see the adult dogs on the breeder's premises, too, to indicate how well she cares for her dogs.

nurturing and a proper canine education to mold him into a responsible, well-behaved canine citizen. Your Saluki's health and good manners will need consistent monitoring and regular "tune-ups," so your job as a responsible dog owner will be ongoing throughout every stage of his life. If you are not prepared to accept these responsibilities and commit to them for the next 15 years, then you are not prepared to own a Saluki, or any other dog.

Although the responsibilities of owning a dog may at times tax your patience, the joy of living with your Saluki far outweighs the workload, and a well-mannered adult dog is worth your time and effort. Before your very eyes, your new charge will grow up to be your most loyal friend, devoted to you unconditionally.

YOUR SALUKI SHOPPING LIST
Just as expectant parents prepare a nursery for their baby, so should you ready your home for the arrival of your Saluki pup. If you have the necessary puppy supplies purchased and in place before he comes home, it will ease the puppy's transition from the

Healthy pups exhibit curiosity, bright eyes and boundless energy.

warmth and familiarity of his mom and littermates to the brand-new environment of his new home and human family. You will be too busy to stock up and prepare your house after your pup comes home, that's for sure! Imagine how a pup must feel upon being transported to a strange new place. It's up to you to comfort him and to let your little pup know that he is going to be happy with you.

FOOD AND WATER BOWLS
Your puppy will need separate bowls for his food and water. Stainless steel pans are generally preferred over plastic bowls since they sterilize better and pups are less inclined to chew on the metal. Heavy-duty ceramic bowls are popular, but consider how often you will have to pick up those heavy bowls. Buy adult-sized pans, as your puppy will grow into them before you know it.

QUALITY FOOD

The cost of food must be mentioned. All dogs need a good-quality food with an adequate supply of protein to develop their bones and muscles properly. Unless fed properly, growing puppies can quickly succumb to health and orthopedic problems.

THE DOG CRATE

If you think that crates are tools of punishment and confinement for when a dog has misbehaved, think again. Although all breeders do not advocate crate training, more and more breeders are recommending the crate as the preferred house-training aid as well as for all-around puppy training and safety. Because dogs are natural den creatures that prefer cave-like environments, the benefits of crate use are many. The crate provides the puppy with his very own "safe house," a cozy place to sleep, take

a break or seek comfort with a favorite toy; a travel aid to house your dog when on the road, at motels or at the vet's office; a training aid to help teach your puppy proper toileting habits; a place of solitude when non-dog people happen to drop by and don't want a lively puppy—or even a well-behaved adult dog—saying hello or begging for attention.

Crates come in several types, although the wire crate and the fiberglass airline-type crate are the most popular. Both are safe and your puppy will adjust to either one, so the choice is up to you. The wire crates offer better visibility for the pup as well as better ventilation. Many of the wire

But Mom, where did our brother go?

Two generations of beauty. Good breeders strive to perpetuate the best qualities of the breed: elegant appearance, keen instincts, typical temperament, sound body and good health.

crates easily collapse into suitcase-size carriers. The fiberglass crates, similar to those used by the airlines for animal transport, are sturdier and more den-like. However, the fiberglass crates do not collapse and are less ventilated than the wire crates, which can be problematic in hot weather. Some of the newer crates are made of heavy plastic mesh; they are very lightweight and fold up into slim-line suitcases. However, mesh crates are only used ringside at shows and agility trials and will not serve to confine a dog reliably unless you are beside the crate.

Don't bother with a puppy-sized crate. Although your Saluki will be a wee fellow when you bring him home, he will grow up in the blink of an eye and your puppy crate will be useless. Purchase a crate that will accommodate an adult Saluki. A large crate will be necessary for a Saluki, who can stand between 23 and 28 inches when fully grown.

The most common crate types: mesh on the left, wire on the right and fiberglass on top.

BEDDING AND CRATE PADS
Your puppy will enjoy some type of soft bedding in his "room" (the crate), something he can snuggle into to feel cozy and secure. Old towels or blankets are good choices for a young pup, since he may (and probably will) have a toileting accident or two in the crate or decide to chew on the bedding material. Once he is fully trained and out of the early chewing stage, you can replace the puppy bedding with a perma-nent crate pad if you prefer. Crate pads and other dog beds run the gamut from inexpensive to high-end doggie-designer styles, but

don't splurge on the good stuff until you are sure that your puppy is reliable and won't tear it up or make a mess on it.

PUPPY TOYS

Just as infants and older children require objects to stimulate their minds and bodies, puppies need toys to entertain their curious brains, wiggly paws and achy teeth. A fun array of safe doggie toys will help satisfy your puppy's chewing instincts and distract him from gnawing on the leg of your antique chair or your new leather sofa. Most puppy toys are cute and look as if they would be a lot of fun, but not all are necessarily safe or good for your puppy, so use caution when you go puppy-toy shopping.

Salukis puppies are fairly aggressive chewers. Like many other dogs, they love to chew. The best "chewcifiers" are nylon and hard rubber bones, which are safe to gnaw on and come in sizes appropriate for all age groups and breeds. Be especially careful of natural bones, which can splinter or develop dangerous sharp edges; pups can easily swallow or choke on those bone splinters. Veterinarians often tell of surgical nightmares involving bits of splintered bone, because in addition to the danger of choking, the sharp pieces can damage the intestinal tract.

Similarly, rawhide chews, while a favorite of most dogs and puppies, can be equally dangerous. Pieces of rawhide are easily swallowed after they get soft and gummy from chewing, and dogs have been known to choke on large pieces of ingested rawhide. Rawhide chews should be offered only when you can supervise the puppy.

CRATE EXPECTATIONS

To make the crate more inviting to your puppy, you can offer his first meal or two inside the crate, always keeping the crate door open so that he does not feel confined. Keep a favorite toy or two in the crate for him to play with while inside. You can also cover the crate at night with a lightweight sheet to make it more den-like and remove the stimuli of household activity. Never put him into his crate as punishment or as you are scolding him, since he will then associate his crate with negative situations and avoid going there.

Soft woolly toys are special puppy favorites. They come in a wide variety of cute shapes and sizes; some look like little stuffed animals. Puppies love to shake them up and toss them about, or simply carry them around. Be careful of fuzzy toys that have button eyes or noses that your pup could chew off and swallow, and make sure that he does not disembowel a squeaky toy to remove the squeaker! Braided rope toys are similar in that they are fun to chew and toss around, but they shred easily and the strings are easy to swallow. The strings are not digestible and, if the puppy doesn't pass them in his stool, he could end up at the vet's office. As with rawhides, your puppy should be closely monitored with rope toys.

If you believe that your pup has ingested a piece of one of his toys, check his stools for the next couple of days to see if he passes the item when he defecates. At the same time, also watch for signs of intestinal distress. A call to your veterinarian might be in order to get his advice and be on the safe side.

An all-time favorite toy for puppies (young and old!) is the empty gallon milk jug. Hard plastic juice containers—46 ounces or more—are also excellent. Such containers make lots of noise when they are batted about, and puppies go crazy with delight as

TOYS 'R SAFE

The vast array of tantalizing puppy toys is staggering. Stroll through any pet shop or pet-supply outlet and you will see that the choices can be overwhelming. However, not all dog toys are safe or sensible. Most very young puppies enjoy soft woolly toys that they can snuggle with and carry around. (You know they have outgrown them when they shred them up!) Avoid toys that have buttons, tabs or other enhancements that can be chewed off and swallowed. Soft toys that squeak are fun, but make sure your puppy does not disembowel the toy and remove (and swallow) the squeaker. Toys that rattle or make noise can excite a puppy, but they present the same danger as the squeaky kind and so require supervision. Hard rubber toys that bounce can also entertain a pup, but make sure that the toy is too big for your pup to swallow.

they play with them. However, they don't often last very long, so be sure to remove and replace them when they get chewed up.

A word of caution about homemade toys: be careful with your choices of non-traditional play objects. Never use old shoes or socks, since a puppy cannot distinguish between the old ones on which he's allowed to chew and the new ones in your closet that are strictly off limits. That principle applies to anything that resembles something that you don't want your puppy to chew up.

COLLARS

A lightweight nylon collar is the best choice for a very young pup. Quick-click collars are easy to put on and remove, and they can be adjusted as the puppy grows. Introduce him to his collar as soon as he comes home to get him accustomed to wearing it. He'll get used to it quickly and won't mind a bit. Make sure that it is snug enough that it won't slip off, yet loose enough to be comfortable for the pup. You should be able to slip two fingers between the collar and his neck. Check the collar often, as puppies grow in spurts, and his

A wire crate affords the dog a view of what's going on around him and allows air to flow through freely. This Saluki, however, would benefit from a crate that enables him to stand comfortably at full height.

TEETHING TIME

All puppies chew. It's normal canine behavior. Chewing just plain feels good to a puppy, especially during the three- to five-month teething period when the adult teeth are breaking through the gums. Rather than attempting to eliminate such a strong natural chewing instinct, you will be more successful if you redirect it and teach your puppy what he may or may not chew. Correct inappropriate chewing with a sharp "No!" and offer him a chew toy, praising him when he takes it. Don't become discouraged. Chewing usually decreases after the adult teeth have come in.

lightweight and not as tempting to chew as a leather lead. You can switch to a 6-foot leather lead after your pup has grown and is used to walking politely on a lead. For initial puppy walks and house-training purposes, you should invest in a shorter lead so that you have more control over the puppy. At first you don't want him wandering too far away from you, and when taking him out for toileting you will want to keep him in the specific area chosen for his potty spot.

Once the Saluki is heel-trained with a traditional leash, you can consider purchasing a retractable lead appropriate for your Saluki's adult size. This type of lead is excellent for walking adult dogs that are already leash-wise. The retractable lead allows the dog to roam farther away from you and explore a wider area when out walking, and also retracts when you need to keep him close to you.

HOME SAFETY FOR YOUR PUPPY

The importance of puppy-proofing cannot be overstated. In addition to making your house comfortable for your Saluki's arrival, you also must make sure that your house is safe for your puppy before you bring him home. There are countless hazards in the owner's personal living environment that a pup can sniff, chew, swallow or destroy. Many are obvious; others are not.

collar can become too tight almost overnight. Since Salukis are notorious runners, an owner's choice of collar is critical. A wide-band collar, known as a sight-hound collar, is the wisest choice for daily walks.

LEASHES

A 6-foot nylon lead is an excellent choice for a young puppy. It is

COLLARING OUR CANINES

The standard flat collar with a buckle or a snap, in leather, nylon or cotton, is widely regarded as the everyday all-purpose collar. If the collar fits correctly, you should be able to fit two fingers between the collar and the dog's neck.

Leather Buckle Collars

Limited-Slip Collar

The martingale, Greyhound or limited-slip collar is preferred by many dog owners and trainers. It is fixed with an extra loop that tightens when pressure is applied to the leash. The martingale collar gets tighter but does not "choke" the dog. The limited-slip collar should only be used for walking and training, not for free play or interaction with another dog. These types of collar should never be left on the dog, as the extra loop can lead to accidents.

Thin nylon choke leads are commonly used on show dogs while in the ring, though they are not practical for everyday use. The ideal collar for a Saluki is the broad-banded sighthound collar, which proves safest for walks since the dog can't easily slip out of it.

The harness, with two or three straps that attach over the dog's shoulders and around his torso, is a humane and safe alternative to the conventional collar. By and large, a well-made harness is virtually escape-proof. Harnesses are available in nylon and mesh and can be outfitted on most dogs, with chest girths ranging from 10 to 30 inches.

Snap-Bolt Choke Collar

Harness

Nylon Collar

Quick-Click Closure

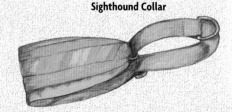

Sighthound Collar

A head collar, composed of a nylon strap that goes around the dog's muzzle and a second strap that wraps around his neck, offers the owner better control over his dog. This device is recommended for problem-solving with dogs (including jumping up, pulling and aggressive behaviors), but must be used with care.

A training halter, including a flat collar and two straps, made of nylon and webbing, is designed for walking. There are several on the market; some are more difficult to put on the dog than others. The halter harness, with two small slip rings at each end, is recommended for ease of use.

A Saluki pup and a child can form a wonderful lasting bond as long as they are taught how to treat each other properly.

house fires that resulted from puppy-chewed electrical cords. Consider this a most serious precaution for your puppy and the rest of your family.

Scout your home for tiny objects that might be seen at a pup's eye level. Keep medication bottles and cleaning supplies well out of reach, and do the same with waste baskets and other trash containers. It goes without saying that you should not use rodent poison or other toxic chemicals in any puppy area and that you must keep such containers safely locked up. You will be amazed at how many places a curious puppy can discover!

Once your house has cleared inspection, check your yard. A

Do a thorough advance house check to remove or rearrange those things that could hurt your puppy, keeping any potentially dangerous items out of areas to which he will have access.

Electrical cords are especially dangerous, since puppies view them as irresistible chew toys. Unplug and remove all exposed cords or fasten them beneath a baseboard where the puppy cannot reach them. Veterinarians and firefighters can tell you horror stories about electrical burns and

KEEP OUT OF REACH

Most dogs don't browse around your medicine cabinet, but accidents do happen! The drug acetaminophen, the active ingredient in certain popular over-the-counter pain relievers, can be deadly to dogs and cats if ingested in large quantities. Acetaminophen toxicity, caused by the dog's swallowing 15 to 20 tablets, can be manifested in abdominal pains within a day or two of ingestion, as well as liver damage. If you suspect your dog has swiped a bottle of pills, get the dog to the vet immediately so that the vet can induce vomiting and cleanse the dog's stomach.

A Dog-Safe Home

The dog-safety police are taking you and your new puppy on a house tour. Let's go room by room and see how safe your own home is for your new pup. The following items are doggie dangers, so either they must be removed or the dog should be monitored or not have access to these areas.

Outdoor
- swimming pool
- pesticides
- toxic plants
- lawn fertilizers

Living Room
- house plants (some varieties are poisonous)
- fireplace or wood-burning stove
- paint on the walls (lead-based paint is toxic)
- lead drapery weights (toxic lead)
- lamps and electrical cords
- carpet cleaners or deodorizers

Bathroom
- blue water in the toilet bowl
- medicine cabinet (filled with potentially deadly bottles)
- soap bars, bleach, drain cleaners, etc.
- tampons

Kitchen
- household cleaners in the kitchen cabinets
- glass jars and canisters
- sharp objects (like kitchen knives, scissors and forks)
- garbage can (with remnants of good-smelling things like onions, potato skins, apple or pear cores, peach pits, coffee beans, etc.)
- "people foods" that are toxic to dogs, like chocolate, raisins, grapes, nuts and onions

Garage
- antifreeze
- fertilizers (including rose foods)
- pesticides and rodenticides
- pool supplies (chlorine and other chemicals)
- oil and gasoline in containers
- sharp objects, electrical cords and power tools

THE GRASS IS ALWAYS GREENER

Must dog owners decide between their beloved canine pals and their perfectly manicured emerald-green lawns? Just as dog urine is no tonic for growing grass, lawn chemicals are extremely dangerous to your dog. Fertilizers, pesticides and herbicides pose real threats to canines and humans alike. Dogs should be kept off treated grounds for at least 24 hours following treatment. Consider some organic options for your lawn care, such as using a homemade compost or a natural fertilizer instead of a commercial chemical. Some dog-conscious lawnkeepers avoid fertilizers entirely, keeping up their lawns by watering, aerating, mowing and seeding frequently.

As always, dogs complicate the equation. Canines love grass. They roll in it, eat it and love to bury their noses in it—and then do their business in it! Grass can mean hours of feel-good, smell-good fun! In addition to the dangers of lawn-care chemicals, there's also the threat of burs, thorns and pebbles in the grass, not to mention the very common grass allergy. Many dogs develop an incurably itchy skin condition from grass, especially in the late summer when the world is in full bloom.

sturdy fence, well embedded into the ground, will give your dog a safe place to play and potty. Salukis are certainly capable of climbing and jumping, as they are very athletic dogs, so a 6-foot-high fence is the minimum requirement to contain an agile youngster or adult. Check the fence periodically for necessary repairs. If there is a weak link or space to squeeze through, you can be sure a determined Saluki will discover it.

The garage and shed can be hazardous places for a pup, as things like fertilizers, chemicals and tools are usually kept there. It's best to keep these areas off-limits to the pup. Antifreeze is especially dangerous to dogs, as they find the taste appealing and it takes only a few licks from the driveway to kill a dog, puppy or adult, small breed or large.

VISITING THE VETERINARIAN

A good veterinarian is your Saluki puppy's best health-insurance policy. If you do not already have a vet, ask friends and experienced dog people in your area for recommendations so that you can select a vet who is experienced with Salukis or at least other sighthounds before you bring your Saluki puppy home. Also arrange for your puppy's first veterinary examination beforehand, since many vets do not have appointments available immediately and your puppy should visit the vet within a day or so of coming home.

It's important to make sure your puppy's first visit to the vet is a pleasant and positive one. The vet should take great care to befriend the pup and handle him gently to make their first meeting a positive experience. The vet will give the pup a thorough physical examination and set up a schedule for vaccinations and other necessary wellness visits. Be sure to show your vet any health and inoculation records, which you should have received from your breeder. Your vet is a great source of canine health information, so be sure to ask questions and take notes. Creating a health journal for your puppy will make a handy reference for his wellness and any future health problems that may arise.

PUPPY PARASITES

Parasites are nasty little critters that live in or on your dog or puppy. Most puppies are born with ascarid roundworms, which are acquired from dormant ascarids residing in the dam. Other parasites can be acquired through contact with infected fecal matter. Take a stool sample to your vet for testing. He will prescribe a safe wormer to treat any parasites found in your puppy's stool. Always have a fecal test performed at your puppy's annual veterinary exam.

MEETING THE FAMILY

Your Saluki's homecoming is an exciting time for all members of the family, and it's only natural that everyone will be eager to meet him, pet him and play with him. However, for the puppy's sake, it's best to make these initial family meetings as uneventful as possible so that the pup is not overwhelmed with too much too soon. Remember, he has just left his dam and his littermates and is away from the breeder's home for the first time. Despite his fuzzy wagging tail, he is still apprehensive and wondering where he is and who all these strange humans are. It's best to let him explore on his own and meet the family members as he feels comfortable. Let him investigate all the new smells, sights and sounds at his own pace. Children should be especially careful to not get overly excited, use loud voices or hug the pup too tightly. Be calm, gentle and affectionate, and

Lounging in luxury, this pampered pup is sure to feel comfortable in his new home.

TOXIC PLANTS

Plants are natural puppy magnets, but many can be harmful, even fatal, if ingested by a puppy or adult dog. Scout your yard and home interior and remove any plants, bushes or flowers that could be even mildly dangerous. It could save your puppy's life. You can obtain a complete list of toxic plants from your veterinarian, at the public library or by looking online.

be ready to comfort him if he appears frightened or uneasy.

Be sure to show your puppy his new crate during this first day home. Toss a treat or two inside the crate; if he associates the crate with food, he will associate the crate with good things. If he is comfortable with the crate, you can offer him his first meal inside it. Leave the door ajar so he can wander in and out as he chooses.

FIRST NIGHT IN HIS NEW HOME

So much has happened in your Saluki puppy's first day away from the breeder. He's had his first car ride to his new home. He's met his new human family and perhaps the other family pets. He has explored his new house and yard, at least those places where he is to be allowed during his first weeks at home. He may have visited his new veterinarian. He has eaten his first meal or two

away from his dam and litter-mates. Surely that's enough to tire out an eight-week-old Saluki pup...or so you hope!

It's bedtime. During the day, the pup investigated his crate, which is his new den and sleeping space, so it is not entirely strange to him. Line the crate with a soft towel or blanket that he can snuggle into and gently place him into the crate for the night. Some breeders send home a piece of bedding from where the pup slept with his littermates, and those familiar scents are a great comfort for the puppy on his first night without his siblings.

He will probably whine or cry. The puppy is objecting to the confinement and the fact that he is alone for the first time. This can be a stressful time for you as well as for the pup. It's important that you remain strong and don't let the puppy out of his crate to comfort him. He will fall asleep eventually. If you release him, the puppy will learn that crying means "out" and will continue that habit. You are laying the groundwork for future bad habits. Some breeders find that soft music can soothe a crying pup and help him get to sleep.

SOCIALIZING YOUR PUPPY

The first 20 weeks of your Saluki puppy's life are the most important of his entire lifetime. A properly socialized puppy will grow up to be a confident and stable adult who will be a pleasure to live with and a welcome addition to the neighborhood.

The importance of socialization cannot be overemphasized; do not hesitate to begin your Saluki's socialization. Research on canine behavior has proven that puppies who are not exposed to new sights, sounds, people and animals during their first 20 weeks of life will grow up to be timid and fearful, even aggressive, and unable to flourish outside of their home environment.

Socializing your puppy is not difficult and, in fact, will be a fun time for you both. Lead training goes hand in hand with socialization, so your puppy will be learning how to walk on a lead at the

FIRST CAR RIDE

The ride to your home from the breeder will no doubt be your puppy's first automobile experience, and you should make every effort to keep him comfortable and secure. Bring a large towel or small blanket for the puppy to lie on during the trip and an extra towel in case the pup gets carsick or has a potty accident. It's best to have another person with you to hold the puppy in his lap. Most puppies will fall fast asleep from the rolling motion of the car. If the ride is lengthy, you may have to stop so that the puppy can relieve himself, so be sure to bring a leash and collar for those stops. Avoid rest areas for potty trips, since those are frequented by many dogs, who may carry parasites or disease. It's better to stop at grassy areas near gas stations or shopping centers to prevent unhealthy exposure for your pup.

Salukis are agile climbers and jumpers. Consider this when designing a fence and ensure that your yard is escape-proof.

same time that he's meeting the neighborhood. Because the Saluki is such a fabulous breed, everyone will enjoy meeting "the new kid on the block." Take him for short walks, to the park and to other dog-friendly places where he will encounter new people, especially children. If your Saluki pup is tentative about meeting strangers, encourage him gently to proceed.

Puppies automatically recognize children as "little people" and are drawn to play with them.

Alert and keen, your eagle-eyed sighthound can spy something that catches his interest at a considerable distance, making safety precautions ever essential.

Be especially careful of your puppy's encounters and experiences during the eight-to-ten-week-old period, which is also called the "fear period." This is a serious imprinting period, and all contact during this time should be gentle and positive. A frightening or negative event could leave a permanent impression that could affect his future behavior if a similar situation arises.

Discuss the timing of your pup's socialization and how to minimize health risks with your breeder, as some breeders recommend socializing the puppy even before he has received all of his inoculations. The belief here is

Just make sure that you supervise these meetings and that the children do not get too rough or encourage him to play too hard. An overzealous pup can often nip too hard, frightening the child and in turn making the puppy overly excited. A bad experience in puppyhood can impact a dog for life, so a pup that has a negative experience with a child may grow up to be shy or even aggressive around children.

Take your puppy along on your daily errands. Puppies are natural "people magnets," and most people who see your pup will want to pet him. All of these encounters will help to mold him into a confident adult dog. Likewise, you will soon feel like a confident, responsible dog owner, rightly proud of your well-mannered Saluki.

that there is a risk of the Saluki's temperament suffering if socialization is delayed.

LEADER OF THE PUPPY'S PACK

Like other canines, your puppy needs an authority figure, someone he can look up to and regard as the leader of his "pack." His first pack leader was his dam, who taught him to be polite and not chew too hard on her ears or nip at her muzzle. He learned those same lessons from his littermates. If he played too rough, they cried in pain and stopped the game, which sent an important message to the rowdy puppy.

CREATE A SCHEDULE

Puppies thrive on sameness and routine. Offer meals at the same time each day, take him out at regular times for potty trips and do the same for play periods and outdoor activity. Make note of when your puppy naps and when he is most lively and energetic, and try to plan his day around those times. Once he is house-trained and more predictable in his habits, he will be better able to tolerate changes in his schedule.

As puppies play together, they are also struggling to determine who will be the boss. Being pack animals, dogs need someone to be in charge. If a litter of puppies remained together beyond puppy-hood, one of the pups would emerge as the strongest one, the one who calls the shots.

Once your puppy leaves the pack, he will look intuitively for a new leader. If he does not recognize you as that leader, he will try to assume that position for himself. Of course, it is hard to imagine your adorable Saluki puppy trying to be in charge when he is so small and seemingly helpless, but watch out! You must remember that these are natural canine instincts. Do not cave in and allow your pup to get the upper "paw."

Just as socialization is so important during these first 20

The proper way for a Saluki (or any other dog) and young friends to greet each other.

REPEAT YOURSELF
Puppies learn best through repetition. Use the same verbal cues and commands when teaching your puppy new behaviors or correcting for misbehaviors. Be consistent, but not monotonous. Puppies get bored just like puppy owners.

weeks, so too is your puppy's early education. He was born without any bad habits. He does not know what is good or bad behavior. If he does things like nipping and digging, it's because he is having fun and doesn't know that humans consider these things as "bad." It's your job to teach him proper puppy manners, and this is the best time to accomplish that...before he has developed bad habits, since it is much more difficult to "unlearn" or correct unacceptable learned behavior than to teach good behavior from the start.

Make sure that all members of the family understand the importance of being consistent when training their new puppy. If you tell the puppy to stay off the sofa and your daughter allows him to cuddle on the couch to watch her favorite television show, your pup will be confused about what he is and is not allowed to do. Have a family conference before your pup comes home so that everyone understands the basic principles of puppy training and the rules you have set forth for the pup, and agrees to follow them.

The old adage that "an ounce of prevention is worth a pound of cure" is especially true when it comes to puppies. It is much easier to prevent inappropriate behavior than it is to change it. It's also easier and less stressful for the pup, since it will keep discipline to a minimum and create a more positive learning environment for him. That, in turn, will also be easier on you!

Here are a few commonsense tips to keep your belongings safe and your puppy out of trouble:

- Keep your closet doors closed and your shoes, socks and other apparel off the floor so your puppy can't get at them.
- Keep a secure lid on the trash container or put the trash where your puppy can't dig into it. He can't damage what he can't reach!
- Supervise your puppy at all times to make sure he is not

Meeting other dogs is a crucial part of the Saluki's social education.

getting into mischief. If he starts to chew the corner of the rug, you can distract him instantly by tossing a toy for him to fetch. You also will be able to whisk him outside when you notice that he is about to piddle on the carpet. If you can't see your puppy, you can't teach him or correct his behavior.

SOLVING PUPPY PROBLEMS

CHEWING AND NIPPING

Nipping at fingers and toes is normal puppy behavior. Chewing is also the way that puppies investigate their surroundings. However, you will have to teach your puppy that chewing anything other than his toys is not acceptable. That won't happen overnight and at times puppy teeth will test your patience. However, if you allow nipping and chewing to continue, just think about the damage that a mature Saluki can do with a full set of adult teeth.

Whenever your puppy nips your hand or fingers, cry out "Ouch!" in a loud voice, which should startle your puppy and stop him from nipping, even if only for a moment. Immediately distract him by offering a small treat or an appropriate toy for him to chew instead (which means having chew toys and puppy treats handy or in your pockets at all times). Praise him when he takes the toy and tell him what a good fellow he is.

DIGGING OUT

Most Saluki dogs love to dig...and are good at it. Digging is considered "self-rewarding behavior" because it's fun! Of all the digging solutions offered by the experts, most are only marginally successful and none is guaranteed to work. The best cure is prevention, which means removing the dog from the offending site when he digs as well as distracting him when you catch him digging so that he turns his attentions elsewhere. That means that you have to supervise your dog's yard time. An unsupervised digger can create havoc with your landscaping or, worse, run away if he digs under a fence.

Enjoying a good scratch from Mom.

pup) during the teething period when the puppy's adult teeth are coming in. At this stage, chewing just plain feels good. Furniture legs and cabinet corners are common puppy favorites. Shoes and other personal items also taste pretty good to a pup.

The best solution is, once again, prevention. If you value something, keep it tucked away and out of reach. You can't hide your dining-room table in a closet, but you can try to deflect the chewing by applying a bitter product made just to deter dogs from chewing. Available in a spray or cream, this substance is vile-tasting, although safe for dogs, and most puppies will avoid the forbidden object after one tiny taste. You also can apply the product to your leather leash if the puppy tries to chew on his lead during leash-training sessions.

Praise is even more important in puppy training than discipline and correction.

Puppies also tend to nip at children more often than adults, since they perceive little ones to be more vulnerable and more similar to their littermates. Teach your children appropriate responses to nipping behavior. If they are unable to handle it themselves, you may have to intervene. Puppy nips can be quite painful and a child's frightened reaction will only encourage a puppy to nip harder, which is a natural canine response. As with all other puppy situations, interaction between your Saluki puppy and children should be supervised.

Chewing on objects, not just family members' fingers and ankles, is also normal canine behavior that can be especially tedious (for the owner, not the

Keep a ready supply of safe chews handy to offer your Saluki as a distraction when he starts to chew on something that's a "no-no." Remember, at this tender age he does not yet know what is permitted or forbidden, so you have to be "on call" every minute he's awake and on the prowl.

You may lose a treasure or two during puppy's growing-up period, and the furniture could sustain a nasty nick or two. These can be trying times, so be prepared for those inevitable accidents and comfort yourself in knowing that this too shall pass.

"COUNTER SURFING"

What we like to call "counter surfing" is normal behavior for tall dogs and usually starts to happen as soon as a puppy realizes that he is big enough to stand on his hind legs and investigate the good stuff on the kitchen counter or the coffee table. Once again, you have to be there to prevent it! As soon as you see your Saluki even start to raise himself up, startle him with a sharp "No!" or "Aaahh, aaahh!" If he succeeds and manages to get one or both paws on the forbidden surface, tell him "Off!" as you gently grasp his paws and guide them back to the floor. As soon as he's back on all four paws, command him to sit and praise at once.

For surf prevention, make sure to keep any tempting treats or edibles out of reach, where your Saluki can't see or smell them. It's the old rule of prevention yet again.

FOOD GUARDING

Some dogs are picky eaters; others eagerly await every meal. Occasionally, the true "chow hound" will become protective of his food, which is one dangerous step toward other aggressive behavior. Food guarding is obvious: your puppy will growl, snarl or even attempt to bite you if you

A sturdy, yet lightweight, collar and lead that your Saluki cannot slip out of are necessary equipment for walking and training your Saluki.

approach his food bowl or put your hand into his pan while he's eating.

This behavior is not acceptable, and very preventable! If your puppy is an especially voracious eater, sit next to him occasionally while he eats and dangle your fingers in his food bowl. Don't feed him in a corner, where he could feel possessive of his eating space. Rather, place his food bowl in an open area of your kitchen where you are in close proximity. Occasionally remove his food in mid-meal, tell him he's a good boy and return his bowl.

If your pup becomes possessive of his food, look for other signs of future aggression, like guarding his favorite toys or refusing to obey obedience commands that he knows. Consult an obedience trainer for help in reinforcing obedience so your Saluki will fully understand that *you* are the boss.

PROPER CARE OF YOUR

SALUKI

Adding a Saluki to your household means adding a new family member who will need your care each and every day. When your Saluki pup first comes home, you will start a routine with him so that, as he grows up, your dog will have a daily schedule just as you do. The aspects of your dog's daily care will likewise become regular parts of your day, so you'll both have a new schedule. Dogs learn by consistency and thrive on routine: regular times for meals, exercise, grooming and potty trips are just as important for your dog as they are to you! Your dog's schedule will depend much on your family's daily routine, but remember that you now have a new member of the family who is part of your day every day.

FEEDING

Feeding your dog the best diet is based on various factors, including age, activity level, overall condition and size of breed. When you visit the breeder, he will share with you his advice about the proper diet for your dog based on his experience with the breed and the foods with which he has had success. Likewise, your vet will be a helpful source of advice throughout the dog's life and will aid you in planning a diet for optimal health.

FEEDING THE PUPPY

Of course, your pup's very first food will be his dam's milk. There may be special situations in which pups fail to nurse, necessitating that the breeder hand-feed them with a formula, but for the most part pups spend the first weeks of life nursing from their dam. The breeder weans the pups by gradually introducing solid foods and decreasing the milk meals. Pups may even start themselves off on the weaning process, albeit inadvertently, if they snatch bites from their mom's food bowl.

By the time the pups are ready for new homes, they are fully weaned and eating a good puppy food. As a new owner, you may be thinking, "Great! The breeder has taken care of the hard part." Not so fast.

A puppy's first year of life is the time when all or most of his growth and development takes place. This is a delicate time, and diet plays a huge role in proper skeletal and muscular formation. Improper diet and exercise habits can lead to damaging problems that will compromise the dog's health and movement for his entire life. That being said, new owners should not worry needlessly. With the myriad types of food formulated specifically for growing pups of different-sized breeds, dog-food manufacturers have taken much of the guesswork out of feeding your puppy well. Since growth-food formulas are designed to provide the nutrition that a growing puppy needs, it is unnecessary and, in fact, can prove harmful to add supplements to the diet. Research has shown that too much of certain vitamin supplements and minerals predispose a dog to skeletal problems. It's by no means a case of "if a little is good, a lot is better." At every stage of your dog's life, too

SWITCHING FOODS

There are certain times in a dog's life when it becomes necessary to switch his food; for example, from puppy to adult food and then from adult to senior-dog food. Additionally, you may decide to feed your pup a different type of food from that received from the breeder, and there may be "emergency" situations in which you can't find your dog's normal brand and have to offer something else temporarily. Anytime a change is made, for whatever reason, the switch must be done gradually. You don't want to upset the dog's stomach or end up with a picky eater who refuses to eat something new. A tried-and-true approach is, over the course of about a week, to mix a little of the new food in with the old, increasing the proportion of new to old as the days progress. At the end of the week, you'll be feeding his regular portions of the new food, and he will barely notice the change.

much or too little in the way of nutrients can be harmful, which is why a manufactured complete food is the easiest way to know that your dog is getting what he needs.

Because of a young pup's small body and accordingly small digestive system, his daily portion will be divided up into small meals throughout the day.

Don't let your pup trick you into giving him a "people food" treat! Some foods can unbalance an otherwise complete diet, cause stomach upset or even be toxic to a dog.

This can mean starting off with three or more meals a day and decreasing the number of meals as the pup matures. For the adult, it is generally thought that dividing the day's food into two meals on a morning/evening schedule, rather than one large daily portion, is healthier for the dog's digestion and reduces the chance of bloat.

Regarding the feeding schedule, feeding the pup at the same times and in the same place each day is important for both housebreaking purposes and establishing the dog's everyday routine. As for the amount to feed, growing puppies generally need proportionately more food per body weight than their adult counterparts, but a pup should never be allowed to gain excess weight. Dogs of all ages should be kept in proper body condition, but extra weight can strain a pup's developing frame, causing skeletal problems.

Watch your pup's weight as he grows and, if the recommended amounts seem to be too much or too little for your pup, consult the vet about appropriate dietary changes. Keep in mind that treats, although small, can quickly add up throughout the day, contributing unnecessary calories. Treats are fine when used prudently; opt for dog treats specially formulated to be healthy or for nutritious snacks like small pieces of cheese or cooked chicken. A quick test to

> **NOT HUNGRY?**
> No dog in his right mind would turn down his dinner, would he? If you notice that your dog has lost interest in his food, there could be any number of causes. Dental problems are a common cause of appetite loss, one that is often overlooked. If your dog has a toothache, a loose tooth or sore gums from infection, chances are it doesn't feel so good to chew. Think about when you've had a toothache! If your dog does not approach the food bowl with his usual enthusiasm, look inside his mouth for signs of a problem. Whatever the cause, you'll want to consult your vet so that your chow hound can get back to his happy, hungry self as soon as possible.

check your dog's weight is to stand behind him and look down. If you can see a clear distinction between the rib and loin areas, without the ribs showing excessively, his weight is ideal.

FEEDING THE ADULT DOG

For the adult (meaning physically mature) dog, feeding properly is about maintenance, not growth. Again, correct weight is a concern. Your dog should appear fit and should have an evident "waist." His ribs should not be protruding (a sign of being underweight), but they should be covered by only a slight layer of fat. Under normal circumstances, an adult dog can be maintained fairly easily with a high-quality nutritionally complete adult-formula food.

Salukis, like all other sighthounds, are very easy keepers and require relatively little food, especially if it is high in protein and fat. Monitor your dog at all times and cut back on his food intake if he appears to be gaining too much weight. Dietary requirements change with the level of activity, the time of year and, in females, the reproductive cycle.

Factor treats into your dog's overall daily caloric intake, and avoid offering table scraps. Not only are some "people foods," like chocolate, onions, grapes, nuts and raisins, toxic to dogs, but feeding from the table encourages begging and overeating. Overweight dogs are more prone to health problems. Research has even shown that obesity takes years off a dog's life. With that in mind, resist the urge to overfeed and over-treat. Don't make unnecessary additions to your dog's diet, whether with tidbits or with extra vitamins and minerals.

The amount of food needed for proper maintenance will vary depending on the individual dog's activity level, but you will be able to tell whether the daily portions are keeping him in good shape. With the wide variety of good complete foods available, choosing what to feed is largely a matter of

personal preference. Just as with the puppy, the adult dog should have consistency in his mealtimes and feeding place. In addition to a consistent routine, regular mealtimes allow the owner to implement bloat preventives like no exercise for at least one hour before and after meals, to see how much his dog is eating. If the dog seems never to be satisfied or, likewise, becomes uninterested in his food, the owner will know right away that something is wrong and can consult the vet.

Keeping a feathered Saluki's hair out of the dinner plate is often accomplished by using a snood.

DIETS FOR THE AGING DOG

A good rule of thumb is that once a dog has reached around 75% of his expected lifespan, he has reached "senior citizen" or geriatric status. Your Saluki will be considered a senior at about 9 or 10 years of age; he has a projected lifespan of about 14 to 15 years.

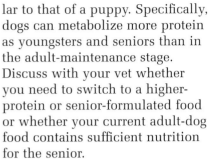

DIET DON'TS

- Got milk? Don't give it to your dog! Dogs cannot tolerate large quantities of cows' milk, as they do not have the enzymes to digest lactose.
- You may have heard of dog owners who add raw eggs to their dogs' food for a shiny coat or to make the food more palatable, but consumption of raw eggs too often can cause a deficiency of the vitamin biotin.
- Avoid feeding table scraps, as they will upset the balance of the dog's complete food. Additionally, fatty or highly seasoned foods can cause upset canine stomachs.
- Do not offer raw meat to your dog. Raw meat can contain parasites; it also is high in fat.
- Vitamin A toxicity in dogs can be caused by too much raw liver, especially if the dog already gets enough vitamin A in his balanced diet, which should be the case.
- Bones like chicken, pork chop and other soft bones are not suitable, as they easily splinter.

What does aging have to do with your dog's diet? No, he won't get a discount at the local diner's early-bird special. Yes, he will require some dietary changes to accommodate the changes that come along with increased age. One change is that the older dog's dietary needs become more similar to that of a puppy. Specifically, dogs can metabolize more protein as youngsters and seniors than in the adult-maintenance stage. Discuss with your vet whether you need to switch to a higher-protein or senior-formulated food or whether your current adult-dog food contains sufficient nutrition for the senior.

Watching the dog's weight remains essential, even more so in the senior stage. Older dogs are already more vulnerable to illness, and obesity only contributes to their susceptibility to problems. As the older dog becomes less active and thus exercises less, his regular portions may cause him to gain weight. At this point, you may consider decreasing his daily food intake or switching to a reduced-calorie food. As with other changes, you should consult your vet for advice.

TYPES OF FOOD AND READING THE LABEL

When selecting the type of food to feed your dog, it is important to check out the label for ingredients. Many dry-food products have soybean, corn or rice as the main ingredient. The main ingredient will be listed first on the label, with the rest of the ingredients following in descending order according to their proportion in the food. While these types of dry food are fine, you should also look into dry foods based on meat or fish. These are better-quality foods and thus higher priced. However, they may be just as economical in the long run, because studies have shown that it takes less of the higher-quality foods to maintain a dog.

Comparing the various types of food, dry, canned and semi-moist, dry foods contain the least amount of water and canned foods the most. Proportionately, dry foods are the most calorie- and nutrient-dense, which means that

The snood can also be used outdoors to keep the ear feathering from getting dirty or picking up debris.

you need more of a canned food product to supply the same amount of nutrition. In households with breeds of disparate size, the canned/dry/semi-moist question can be of special importance. Larger breeds obviously eat more than smaller ones and thus in general do better on dry foods, but smaller breeds do fine on canned foods and require "small bite" formulations to protect their small mouths and teeth if fed dry foods. So if you have breeds of different sizes in your household, consider both your own preferences and what your dogs like to eat, but generally think canned for the little guys and dry or semi-moist for everyone else. You may find success mixing the food types as well. Water is important for all dogs, but even more so for those fed dry foods, as there is not much water content in their food.

There are strict controls that regulate the nutritional content of dog food, and a food has to meet

THINK BEFORE YOU BARF

There are many fans of the Biologically Appropriate Raw Food (BARF) diet made famous by Dr. Ian Billinghurst. There are also numerous other home-prepared diets, each of which has its own coterie of adherents. All of these owners will attest that their dogs' health has improved dramatically when switched from commercial dog food. While this may the case for a few, the vast majority of dogs fed on one of these diets is unhealthy, due to a lack of one or more critical nutrients or vitamins. If you want to try one of these diets, it is highly recommended that you submit the diet to an analytical laboratory to determine if, in fact, everything the dog needs is contained in the diet. (One such laboratory is found online at www.petdiets.com.)

Elevated bowls, once thought to reduce the likelihood of bloat, have been shown to increase the frequency of bloat.

The food label may also make feeding suggestions, such as whether moistening a dry-food product is recommended. Sometimes a splash of water will make the food more palatable for the dog and even enhance the flavor. Adding some water to dry food is also advised as a bloat preventive.

Don't be overwhelmed by the many factors that go into feeding your dog. Manufacturers of complete and balanced foods make it easy, and once you find the right food and amounts for your Saluki, his daily feeding will be a matter of routine.

the minimum requirements in order to be considered "complete and balanced." It is important that you choose such a food for your dog, so check the label to be sure that your chosen food meets the requirements. If not, look for a food that clearly states on the label that it is formulated to be complete and balanced for your dog's particular stage of life.

Recommendations for amounts to feed will be indicated on the label. You should also ask your vet about proper food portions, and you will keep an eye on your dog's condition to see whether the recommended amounts are adequate. If he becomes over- or underweight, you will need to make adjustments; this also would be a good time to consult your vet.

DON'T FORGET THE WATER!
For a dog, it's always time for a drink! Regardless of what type of food he eats, there's no doubt that he needs plenty of water. Fresh cold water, in a clean bowl, should be freely available to your dog at all times. There are special circumstances, such as during puppy housebreaking, when you will want to monitor your pup's water intake so that you will be able to predict when he will need to relieve himself, but water must be available to him nonetheless. Water is essential for hydration and proper body function just as it is in humans.

You will get to know how much your dog typically drinks in a day. Of course, in the heat or if exercising vigorously, he will be more thirsty and will drink more. However, if he begins to drink noticeably more water for no apparent reason, this could signal any of various problems, and you are advised to consult your vet.

A word of caution concerning your deep-chested dog's water intake: he should never be allowed to gulp water, especially at mealtimes. In fact, his water intake should be limited at mealtimes as a rule. This simple daily precaution can go a long way in protecting your dog from the dangerous and potentially fatal gastric torsion (bloat).

EXERCISE

Salukis are much more active dogs than most. They have very

Is there anything more graceful than a Saluki running at top speed? Seeing these Salukis in action is indicative of how much exercise the breed requires.

PUPPY STEPS

Puppies are brimming with activity and enthusiasm. It seems that they can play all day and night without tiring, but don't overdo your puppy's exercise regimen. Easy does it for the puppy's first six to nine months. Keep walks brief and don't let the puppy engage in stressful jumping games. The puppy frame is delicate, and too much exercise during those critical growing months can cause injury to his bone structure, ligaments and musculature. Save his first jog for his first birthday!

high energy levels and require considerable amounts of exercise on a daily basis. Long walks off lead in safe areas are the best exercise, but you must be very careful. Salukis are sighthounds and will chase anything that moves, including the neighbor's cat. When off lead, they may chase deer or any other animal for miles. Their speed and endurance are characteristics of this breed that are far superior to those of most other dogs. When in the chase mode, a Saluki is unlikely to respond to a recall

TIPS FOR OUTDOOR SAFETY

- The importance of water for your dog cannot be stressed enough. He always needs a bowl of fresh clean water available, indoors and out. Dogs lose a lot of hydration when panting, and water is the only way to replace it.
- Children can be great playmates for dogs, but do not leave young children and dogs in the yard unattended. A dog can be overexcited by youngsters' boisterous play, causing him to act hyper or otherwise inappropriately.
- Your fenced yard must be a safe play place for your dog. Aside from making it escape-proof for him, keep it locked so that no one can let him out of the yard or enter without your knowledge.
- Never allow the dog to rush outdoors, possibly into danger. Have him sit/stay and wait for your command. If exiting into a non-fenced area, have him on lead. The dog will naturally follow the kids outside, so if the dog is to stay indoors, he should be put into his secure area before doors are opened.
- Keep your canine first-aid kit fully stocked and close at hand, along with emergency phone numbers. Problems encountered outdoors, such as injuries, heat-related issues, bee stings and the like, all require immediate care and veterinary attention.

(come) command. Some sort of organized coursing or racing event is the best place to exercise your Saluki, and daily off-lead runs should be kept to safely enclosed areas.

Although obesity is rarely a problem with Salukis, bear in mind that an overweight dog should never be suddenly over-exercised; instead he should be allowed to increase exercise slowly. Also remember that not only is exercise essential to keep the dog's body fit, it is essential to his mental well-being. A bored dog will find something to do, which often manifests itself in some type of destructive behavior.

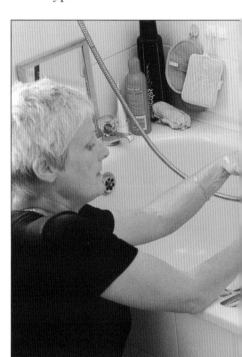

In this sense, it is just as essential for the owner's mental well-being!

GROOMING

BRUSHING

A natural bristle brush or a hound glove can be used for regular routine brushing. Daily brushing is effective for removing dead hair and stimulating the dog's natural oils to add shine and a healthy look to the coat. Although the smooth Saluki's coat is short and close, it does require regular five-minute once-overs to keep it looking its shiny best. The feathered Saluki requires more extensive grooming, although the silkiness

WATER SHORTAGE
No matter how well behaved your dog is, bathing is always a project! Nothing can substitute for a good warm bath, but owners do have the option of giving their dogs "dry" baths. Pet shops sell excellent products, in both powder and spray forms, designed for spot-cleaning your dog. These dry shampoos are convenient for touch-up jobs when you don't have the time to bathe your dog in the traditional way.

Muddy feet, messy behinds and smelly coats can be spot-cleaned and deodorized with a "wet-nap"-style cleaner. On those days when your dog insists on rolling in fresh goose droppings and there's no time for a bath, a spot bath can save the day. These pre-moistened wipes are also handy for other grooming needs like wiping faces, ears and eyes and freshening tails and behinds.

Regular bathing is essential for healthy skin and a gleaming coat. Only use shampoos made especially for dogs, and thoroughly wet the Saluki's coat before soaping up.

of the hair reduces the likelihood of matting. Regular grooming sessions are also a good way to spend time with your dog. Many dogs grow to like the feel of being brushed and will enjoy the routine.

BATHING

In general, dogs need to be bathed only a few times a year, possibly more often if your dog gets into something messy or if he starts to smell like a dog.

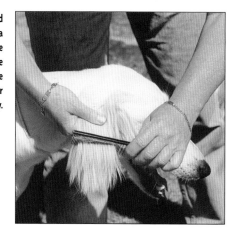

A fine-toothed comb and a gentle touch are needed for the long hair on the ears and other parts of the body.

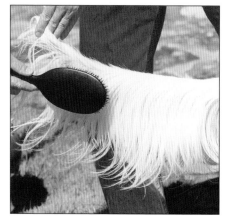

The Saluki's tail can be brushed out gently with a brush.

A special brush like this serves a dual purpose: it adds shine to the coat while the rubber knobs massage the dog as you groom, making grooming a more enjoyable experience for the Saluki.

Show dogs are usually bathed before every show, which could be as frequent as weekly, although this depends on the owner. Bathing too frequently can have negative effects on the skin and coat, removing natural oils and causing dryness.

If you give your dog his first bath when he is young, he will become accustomed to the process. Wrestling a dog into the tub or chasing a freshly shampooed dog who has escaped from the bath will be no fun! Most dogs don't naturally enjoy their baths, but you at least want yours to cooperate with you.

Before bathing the dog, have the items you'll need close at hand. First, decide where you will bathe the dog. You should have a tub or basin with a non-slip surface. In warm weather, some like to use a portable pool in the yard, although you'll want to make sure your dog doesn't head for the nearest dirt pile following his bath! You will also need a hose or shower spray to wet the coat thoroughly, a shampoo formulated for dogs, absorbent towels and perhaps a blow dryer. Human shampoos are too harsh for dogs' coats and will dry them out.

Before wetting the dog, give him a brush-through to remove any dead hair, dirt and mats. Make sure he is at ease in the tub and have the water at a comfortable temperature. Begin bathing by wetting the coat all the way down to the skin. Massage in the shampoo, keeping it away from his face and eyes. Rinse him thoroughly, again avoiding the eyes and ears, as you don't want to get water into the ear canals. A thorough rinsing is important, as shampoo residue is drying and itchy to the dog. After rinsing, wrap him in a towel to absorb the initial moisture. You can finish drying with either a towel or a blow dryer on low heat, held at a safe distance from the dog. You should keep the dog indoors and away from drafts until he is completely dry.

NAIL CLIPPING

Having his nails trimmed is not on many dogs' lists of favorite things to do. With this in mind, you will need to accustom your puppy to the procedure at a young age so that he will sit still (well, as still as he can) for his pedicures. Long nails can cause the dog's feet to spread, which is not good for him; likewise, long nails can hurt if they unintentionally scratch, not good for you!

Some dogs' nails are worn down naturally by regular walking on hard surfaces, so the frequency with which you clip depends on your individual dog. Look at his nails from time to time and clip as needed; a good way to know when it's time for a trim is if you

hear your dog clicking as he walks across the floor.

There are several types of nail clippers and even electric nail-grinding tools made for dogs; first we'll discuss using the clipper. To start, have your clipper ready and some doggie treats on hand. You want your pup to view his nail-clipping sessions in a positive light, and what better way to convince him than with food? You may want to enlist the help of an assistant to comfort the pup and offer treats as you concentrate on the clipping itself. The guillotine-type clipper is thought of by many as the easiest type to use; the nail tip is inserted into the opening, and blades on the bottom snip it off in one clip. However, this squashes the nail and can hurt the dog. Scissor-type clippers are usually a better choice.

Start by grasping the pup's paw; a little pressure on the foot pad causes the nail to extend,

Once the dog is thoroughly rinsed, use a heavy towel to start drying.

offer a piece of treat with each nail. You can also use nail-clipping time to examine the footpads, making sure that they are not dry and cracked and that nothing has become embedded in them.

The nail grinder, the other choice, is many owners' first choice. Accustoming the puppy to the sound of the grinder and

Whatever tool you use for clipping your Saluki's nails, take it slow and take off just a small piece of nail with each clip.

making it easier to clip. Clip off a little at a time. If you can see the "quick," which is a blood vessel that runs through each nail, you will know how much to trim, as you do not want to cut into the quick. On that note, if you do cut the quick, which will cause bleeding, you can stem the flow of blood with a styptic pencil or other clotting agent. If you mistakenly nip the quick, do not panic or fuss, as this will cause the pup to be afraid. Simply reassure the pup, stop the bleeding and move on to the next nail. Don't be discouraged; you will become a professional canine pedicurist with practice.

You may or may not be able to see the quick, so it's best to just clip off a small bit at a time. If you see a dark dot in the center of the nail, this is the quick and your cue to stop clipping. Tell the puppy he's a "good boy" and

SCOOTING HIS BOTTOM

Here's a doggy problem that many owners tend to neglect. If your dog is scooting his rear end around the carpet, he probably is experiencing anal-sac impaction or blockage. The anal sacs are the two grape-sized glands on either side of the dog's vent. The dog cannot empty these glands, which become filled with a foul-smelling material. The dog may attempt to lick the area to relieve the pressure. He may also rub his anus on your walls, furniture or floors.

Don't neglect your dog's rear end during grooming sessions. By squeezing both sides of the anus with a soft cloth, you can express some of the material in the sacs. If the material is pasty and thick, you likely will need the assistance of a veterinarian. Vets know how to express the glands and can show you how to do it correctly without hurting the dog or spraying yourself with the unpleasant liquid.

THE EARS KNOW

Examining your puppy's ears helps ensure good internal health. The ears are the eyes to the dog's innards! Begin handling your puppy's ears when he's still young so that he doesn't protest every time you lift a flap or touch his ears. Yeast and bacteria are two of the culprits that you can detect by examining the ear. You will notice a strong, often foul, odor, debris, redness or some kind of discharge. All of these point to health problems that can worsen over time. Additionally, you are on the lookout for wax accumulation, ear mites and other tiny bothersome parasites and their even tinier droppings. You may have to pluck hair with tweezers in order to have a better view into the dog's ears, but this is painless if done carefully.

ing has occurred, there are various cleaning agents made especially for this purpose. Look at the dog's eyes to make sure no debris has entered; dogs with large eyes and those who spend time outdoors are especially prone to this.

The signs of an eye infection are obvious: mucus, redness, puffiness, scabs or other signs of irritation. If your dog's eyes become infected, the vet will likely prescribe an antibiotic ointment for treatment. If you notice signs of more serious problems, such as opacities in the eye, which usually indicate cataracts, consult the vet at once. Taking time to pay attention to your dog's eyes will alert you in the early stages of any problem so that you can get your dog treatment as soon as possible. You could save your dog's sight!

sensation of the buzz presents fewer challenges than the clipper, and there's no chance of cutting through the quick. Use the grinder on a low setting and always talk soothingly to your dog. He won't mind his salon visit, and he'll have nicely polished nails as well.

EYE CARE

During grooming sessions, pay extra attention to the condition of your dog's eyes. If the area around the eyes is soiled or if tear stain-

ID FOR YOUR DOG

You love your Saluki and want to keep him safe. Of course you take every precaution to prevent his escaping from the yard or becoming lost or stolen. You have a sturdy high fence and you always keep your dog on lead when out and about in public places. If your dog is not properly identified, however, you are overlooking a major aspect of his safety. We hope to never be in a situation where our dog is missing, but we should practice prevention in the unfortunate case that this

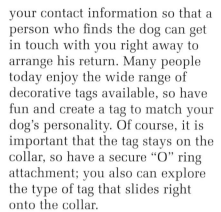

your contact information so that a person who finds the dog can get in touch with you right away to arrange his return. Many people today enjoy the wide range of decorative tags available, so have fun and create a tag to match your dog's personality. Of course, it is important that the tag stays on the collar, so have a secure "O" ring attachment; you also can explore the type of tag that slides right onto the collar.

In addition to the ID tag, which every dog should wear even if identified by another method, two other forms of identification have become popular: microchipping and tattooing. In microchipping, a tiny scannable chip is painlessly inserted under the dog's skin. The number is registered to you so that, if your lost dog turns up at a clinic or shelter, the chip can be scanned to retrieve your contact information.

The advantage of the microchip is that it is a permanent form of ID, but there are some factors to consider. Several different companies make microchips, and not all are compatible with the others' scanning devices. It's best to find a company with a universal microchip that can be read by scanners made by other companies as well. It won't do any good to have the dog chipped if the information cannot be retrieved. Also, not every humane society, shelter and clinic is

You should never drive with your Saluki loose within the vehicle. Always use a crate or other restraint for the safety of all concerned—canine and human.

happens; identification greatly increases the chances of your dog's being returned to you.

There are several ways to identify your dog. First, the traditional dog tag should be a staple in your dog's wardrobe, attached to his everyday collar. Tags can be made of sturdy plastic and various metals and should include

PET OR STRAY?
Besides the obvious benefit of providing your contact information to whoever finds your lost dog, an ID tag makes your dog more approachable and more likely to be recovered. A strange dog wandering the neighborhood without a collar and tags will look like a stray, while the collar and tags indicate that the dog is someone's pet. Even if the ID tags become detached from the collar, the collar alone will make a person more likely to pick up the dog.

CAR CAUTION

You may like to bring your canine companion along on the daily errands, but if you will be running in and out from place to place and can't bring him indoors with you, leave him at home. Your dog should never be left alone in the car, not even for a minute—never! A car heats up very quickly, and even a cracked-open window will not help. In fact, leaving the window cracked will be dangerous if the dog becomes uncomfortable and tries to escape, and it could attract dog thieves. When in doubt, leave your dog home, where you know he will be safe.

equipped with a scanner, although more and more facilities are equipping themselves. In fact, many shelters microchip dogs that they adopt out to new homes.

Because the microchip is not visible to the eye, the dog must wear a tag that states that he is microchipped so that whoever picks him up will know to have him scanned. He of course also

should have a tag with contact information in case his chip cannot be read. Humane societies and veterinary clinics offer microchipping service, which is usually very affordable.

Though less popular than microchipping, tattooing is another permanent method of ID for dogs. Most vets perform this service, and there are also clinics that perform dog tattooing. This is also an affordable procedure and one that will not cause much discomfort for the dog. It is best to put the tattoo in a visible area, such as inside the ear flap, to deter theft. It is sad to say that there are cases of dogs' being stolen and sold to research laboratories, but such laboratories will not accept tattooed dogs.

To ensure that the tattoo is effective in aiding your dog's return to you, the tattoo number must be registered with a national organization. That way, when someone finds a tattooed dog, a phone call to the registry will quickly match the dog with his owner.

It doesn't take much for a sighthound to go off and running, making safety precautions and proper ID essential for your Saluki.

No matter what type of collar your Saluki is wearing, an ID tag is a must.

TRAINING YOUR

SALUKI

LEADER OF THE PACK

Canines are pack animals. They live according to pack rules, and every pack has only one leader. Guess what? That's you! To establish your position of authority, lay down the rules and be fair and good-natured in all your dealings with your dog. He will consider young children as his littermates, but the one who trains him, who feeds him, who grooms him, who expects him to come into line, that's his leader. And he who leads must be obeyed.

BASIC TRAINING PRINCIPLES: PUPPY VS. ADULT

There's a big difference between training an adult dog and training a young puppy. With a young puppy, everything is new. At eight to ten weeks of age, he will be experiencing many things, and he has nothing with which to compare these experiences. Up to this point, he has been with his dam and littermates, not one-on-one with people except in his interactions with his breeder and visitors to the litter.

When you first bring the puppy home, he is eager to please you. This means that he accepts doing things your way. During the next couple of months, he will absorb the basis of everything he needs to know for the rest of his life. This early age is even referred to as the "sponge" stage. After that, for the next 18 months, it's up to you to reinforce good manners by building on the foundation that you've established. Once your puppy is reliable in basic commands and behavior and has reached the appropriate age, you may gradually introduce him to some of the interesting sports, games and activities available to pet owners and their dogs.

Raising your puppy is a family affair. Each member of the family must know what rules to set forth for the puppy and how to use the same one-word commands to mean exactly the same thing every time. Even if yours is a large family, one person will soon be considered by the pup to be the leader, the Alpha person in his pack, the "boss" who must be obeyed. Often that highly regarded person turns out to be the one who feeds the puppy. Food ranks very high on the puppy's list of important things! That's why your puppy is rewarded with small treats along with verbal praise when he

A proper sit in the heel position.

BASIC PRINCIPLES OF DOG TRAINING

1. Start training early. A young puppy is ready, willing and able.
2. Timing is your all-important tool. Praise at the exact time that the dog responds correctly. Pay close attention.
3. Patience is almost as important as timing!
4. Repeat! The same word has to mean the same thing every time.
5. In the beginning, praise all correct behavior verbally, along with treats and petting.

responds to you correctly. As the puppy learns to do what you want him to do, the food rewards are gradually eliminated and only the praise remains. If you were to keep up with the food treats, you could have two problems on your hands—an obese dog and a beggar.

Training begins the minute your Saluki puppy steps through the doorway of your home, so don't make the mistake of putting

the puppy on the floor and telling him by your actions to "Go for it! Run wild!" Even if this is your first puppy, you must act as if you know what you're doing: be the boss. An uncertain pup may be terrified to move, while a bold one will be ready to take you at your word and start plotting to destroy the house! Before you collected your puppy, you decided where his own special place would be, and that's where to put him when you first arrive home. Give him a house tour after he has investigated his area and had a nap and a bathroom "pit stop."

It's worth mentioning here that if you've adopted an adult dog that is completely trained to your liking, lucky you! You're off the hook! However, if that dog spent his life up to this point in a kennel, or even in a good home but without any real training, be prepared to tackle the job ahead. A dog three years of age or older with no previous training cannot be blamed for not knowing what he was never taught. While the dog is trying to understand and learn your rules, at the same time he has to unlearn many of his previously self-taught habits and general view of the world.

Working with a professional trainer will speed up your progress with an adopted adult dog. You'll need patience, too. Some new rules may be close to

BE UPSTANDING!

You are the dog's leader. During training, stand up straight so your dog looks up at you, and therefore up *to* you. Say the command words distinctly, in a clear, declarative tone of voice. (No barking!) Give rewards only as the correct response takes place (remember your timing!). Praise, smiles and treats are "rewards" used to positively reinforce correct responses. Don't repeat a mistake. Just change to another exercise—you will soon find success!

impossible for the dog to accept. After all, he's been successful so far by doing everything his way! (Patience again.) He may agree with your instruction for a few days and then slip back into his old ways, so you must be just as consistent and understanding in your teaching as you would be with a puppy. (More patience needed yet again!) Your dog has to learn to pay attention to your voice, your family, the daily routine, new smells, new sounds and, in some cases, even a new climate.

One of the most important things to find out about a newly adopted adult dog is his reaction to children (yours and others), strangers and your friends, and how he acts upon meeting other dogs. If he was not socialized with dogs as a puppy, this could be a major problem. This does not mean that he's a "bad" dog, a vicious dog or an aggressive dog; rather, it means that he has no idea how to read another dog's body language. There's no way for him to tell whether the other dog is a friend or foe. Survival instinct takes over, telling him to attack first and ask questions later. This definitely calls for professional help and, even then, may not be a behavior that can be corrected 100% reliably (or even at all). If you have a puppy, this is why it is so very important to introduce your young puppy properly to other puppies and "dog-friendly" adult dogs.

Many feel that in order to preserve the nature of this ancient dog, the Saluki must be "free." Free to do as they please? Free to run off? Free to destroy your house? Obviously, in order to live in today's society with a family, dogs must be trained. Remember, the leading cause of death in dogs is automobiles, and this is no different for Salukis than for any other sighthound. To prevent this, fences and training are of utmost importance.

Dogs will be dogs, especially when there's food concerned! Stealing food and begging at the table are two behaviors that must be discouraged early on.

Don't skimp on the praise and petting to let your Saluki know that he's a good dog.

HOUSE-TRAINING YOUR SALUKI

Dogs are tactility-oriented when it comes to house-training. In other words, they respond to the surface on which they are given approval to eliminate. The choice is yours (the dog's version is in parentheses): The lawn (including the neighbors' lawns)? A bare patch of earth under a tree (where people like to sit and relax in the summertime)? Concrete steps or patio (all sidewalks, garages and basement floors)? The curbside (watch out for cars)? A small area of crushed stone in a corner of the yard (mine!)? The latter is the best choice if you can manage it, because it will remain strictly for the dog's use and is easy to keep clean. Indoor training usually means training your dog to newspaper, but training a dog such as a Saluki indoors is self-defeating! They do not melt in the rain...always train your dog to go outside from the very beginning.

WHEN YOUR PUPPY'S "GOT TO GO"
Your puppy's need to relieve himself is seemingly non-stop, but signs of improvement will be seen each week. From 8 to 10 weeks old, the puppy will have to be taken outside every time he wakes up, about 10–15 minutes after every meal and after every period of play—all day long, from first thing in the morning until his bedtime! That's a total of ten or more trips per day to teach the puppy where it's okay to relieve himself. With that schedule in mind, you can see that house-training a young puppy is not a part-time job. It requires someone to be home all day.

If that seems overwhelming or impossible, do a little planning. For example, plan to pick up your puppy at the start of a vacation period. If you can't get home in the middle of the day, plan to hire a dog-sitter or ask a neighbor to come over to take the pup outside, feed him his lunch and then take him out again about ten or so minutes after he's eaten. Also make arrangements with that or another person to be your "emergency" contact if you have to stay late on the job. Remind yourself—

Canine Development Schedule

It is important to understand how and at what age a puppy develops into adulthood. If you are a puppy owner, consult this Canine Development Schedule to determine the stage of development your puppy is currently experiencing. This knowledge will help you as you work with the puppy in the weeks and months ahead.

Period	Age	Characteristics
First to Third	Birth to Seven Weeks	Puppy needs food, sleep and warmth and responds to simple and gentle touching. Needs mother for security and disciplining. Needs littermates for learning and interacting with other dogs. Pup learns to function within a pack and learns pack order of dominance. Begin socializing pup with adults and children for short periods. Pup begins to become aware of his environment.
Fourth	Eight to Twelve Weeks	Brain is fully developed. Pup needs socializing with outside world. Remove from mother and littermates. Needs to change from canine pack to human pack. Human dominance necessary. Fear period occurs between 8 and 12 weeks. Avoid fright and pain.
Fifth	Thirteen to Sixteen Weeks	Training and formal obedience should begin. Less association with other dogs, more with people, places, situations. Period will pass easily if you remember this is pup's change-to-adolescence time. Be firm and fair. Flight instinct prominent. Permissiveness and over-disciplining can do permanent damage. Praise for good behavior.
Juvenile	Four to Eight Months	Another fear period about 7 to 8 months of age. It passes quickly, but be cautious of fright and pain. Sexual maturity reached. Dominant traits established. Dog should understand sit, down, come and stay by now.

Note: These are approximate time frames. Allow for individual differences in puppies.

repeatedly—that this hectic schedule improves as the puppy gets older. As a trained adult, your Saluki should do fine with four daily relief trips.

HOME WITHIN A HOME

Your Saluki puppy needs to be confined to one secure, puppy-proof area when no one is able to watch his every move. Generally, the kitchen is the place of choice because the floor is washable. Likewise, it's a busy family area that will accustom the pup to a variety of noises, everything from pots and pans to the telephone, blender and dishwasher. Puppies are social animals, especially pack dogs like Salukis, and need to feel a part of the pack right from the

I WILL FOLLOW YOU
Obedience isn't just a classroom activity. In your home you have many great opportunities to teach your dog polite manners. Allowing your pet on the bed or furniture elevates him to your level, which is not a good idea (the word is "Off!"). Use the "umbilical cord" method, keeping your dog on lead so he has to go with you wherever you go. You sit, he sits. You walk, he heels. You stop, he sit/stays. Everywhere you go, he's with you, but you go first!

start. He will also be enchanted by the smell of your cooking (and will never be critical when you burn something). An exercise pen (also called an "ex-pen," a puppy version of a playpen) within the room of choice is an excellent means of confinement for a young pup. He can see out and has a certain amount of space in which to run about, but he is safe from dangerous things like electrical cords, heating units, trash baskets or open kitchen-supply cabinets. Place the pen where the puppy will not get a blast of heat or air conditioning.

In the pen, you can put a few toys, his bed (which can be his crate if the dimensions of pen and crate are compatible) and a few layers of newspaper in one small corner, just in case. A water bowl

chase the first few times. At night, after he's been outside, he should sleep in his crate. The crate may be kept in his designated area at night or, if you want to be sure to hear those wake-up yips in the morning, put the crate in a corner of your bedroom. However, don't make any response whatsoever to whining or crying. If he's completely ignored, he'll settle down and get to sleep.

Good bedding for a young puppy is an old folded bath towel

Once reliably trained to relieve himself outdoors, your Saluki will always return to the same area of the yard.

can be hung at a convenient height on the side of the ex-pen so it won't become a splashing pool for an innovative puppy. His food dish can go on the floor, near but not under the water bowl.

Crates are something that pet owners are at last getting used to for their dogs. Wild or domestic canines have always preferred to sleep in den-like safe spots, and that is exactly what the crate provides. How often have you seen adult dogs that choose to sleep under a table or chair even though they have full run of the house? It's the den connection.

In your "happy" voice, use the word "Crate" (or "Kennel" or "House," whatever you choose) every time you put the pup into his den. If he's new to a crate, toss in a small biscuit for him to

LEASH TRAINING

House-training and leash training go hand in hand, literally. When taking your puppy outside to do his business, lead him there on his leash. Unless an emergency potty run is called for, do not whisk the puppy up into your arms and take him outside. If you have a fenced yard, you have the advantage of letting the puppy loose to go out, but it's better to put the dog on the leash and take him to his designated place in the yard until he is reliably house-trained. Taking the puppy for a walk is the best way to house-train a dog. The dog will associate the walk with his time to relieve himself, and the exercise of walking stimulates the dog's bowels and bladder. Dogs that are not trained to relieve themselves on a walk may hold it until they get back home, which of course defeats half the purpose of the walk.

or an old blanket, something that is easily washable and disposable if necessary ("accidents" will happen!). Never put newspaper in the puppy's crate. Also those old ideas about adding a clock to replace his mother's heartbeat, or a hot-water bottle to replace her warmth, are just that—old ideas. The clock could drive the puppy nuts, and the hot-water bottle could end up as a very soggy waterbed! An extremely good breeder would have introduced your puppy to the crate by letting two pups sleep together for a couple of nights, followed by several nights alone. How thankful you will be if you found that breeder!

Your puppy should always sleep in his crate. Many Saluki breeders feel that crates interfere with the proper development of the Saluki mystique. In my expe-

There's so much for inquisitive hounds to explore when out on walks.

SOMEBODY TO BLAME

House-training a puppy can be frustrating for the puppy and the owner alike. The puppy does not instinctively understand the difference between defecating on the pavement outside and on the ceramic tile in the kitchen. He is confused and frightened by his human's exuberant reactions to his natural urges. The owner, arguably the more intelligent of the duo, is also frustrated that he cannot convince his puppy to obey his commands and instructions.

In frustration, the owner may struggle with the temptation to discipline the puppy, scold him or even strike him on the rear end. Shouting and smacking the puppy may make you feel better, but it will defeat your purpose in gaining your puppy's trust and respect. Don't blame your nine-week-old puppy. Blame yourself for not being 100% consistent in the puppy's lessons and routine. The lesson here is simple: try harder and your puppy will succeed.

rience, this is not a detriment to the dog's personality in any way.

Safe toys in the pup's crate or area will keep him occupied, but monitor their condition closely. Discard any toys that show signs of being chewed to bits. Squeaky parts, bits of stuffing or plastic or any other small pieces can cause intestinal blockage or possibly choking if swallowed.

PROGRESSING WITH POTTY-TRAINING

After you've taken your puppy out and he has relieved himself in the area you've selected, he can have some free time with the family as long as there is someone responsible for watching him. That doesn't mean just someone in the same room who is watching TV or busy on the computer, but one person who is doing nothing other than keeping an eye on the pup, playing with him on the floor and helping him understand his position in the pack.

This first taste of freedom will let you begin to set the house rules. If you don't want the dog on the furniture, now is the time to prevent his first attempts to jump up onto the couch. The word to use in this case is "Off," not "Down." "Down" is the word you will use to teach the down position, which is something entirely different.

Most corrections at this stage come in the form of simply distracting the puppy. Instead of

telling him "No" for "Don't chew the carpet," distract the chomping puppy with a toy and he'll forget about the carpet.

As you are playing with the pup, do not forget to watch him closely and pay attention to his body language. Whenever you see him begin to circle or sniff, take the puppy outside to relieve himself. Praise him as he eliminates while he actually is *in the act* of relieving himself. Three seconds after he has finished is too late! You'll be praising him for running toward you, or picking up a toy or whatever he may be doing at that moment, and that's not what you want to be praising him for. Timing is a vital tool in all dog training. Use it.

By always leading pup to the same area, and by pup's following his keen nose, he will quickly learn where his chosen relief spot

Your Saluki should behave well on leash for all members of the family so that everyone can take turns with potty-trip duties.

WATCH THE WATER

To help your puppy sleep through the night without having to relieve himself, remove his water bowl after 7 p.m. Offer him a couple of ice cubes during the evening to quench his thirst. Never leave water in a puppy's crate, as this is inviting puddles of mishaps.

By the time your Saluki is an adult, the potty routine will be just that—routine.

looking at you, but remember that this is neither playtime nor time for a walk. This is strictly a business trip! Then, as he circles and squats (remember your timing!), give him a quiet "Good dog" as praise. If you start to jump for joy, ecstatic over his performance, he'll do one of two things: either he will stop mid-stream, as it were, or he'll do it again for you—in the house—and expect you to be just as delighted!

Give him five minutes or so and, if he doesn't go in that time, take him back indoors to his confined area and try again in

is. That scent attraction is why it's so important to clean up any messes made in the house by using a product specially made to eliminate the odor of dog urine and droppings. If pup can smell remnants of his accident, he will be attracted to that area to use again. Regular household cleansers won't do the trick. Pet shops sell the best pet deodorizers. Invest in the largest container you can find.

When you take your puppy outside to relieve himself, use a one-word command such as "Outside" or "Go-potty" (that's one word to the puppy!) as you pick him up and attach his leash. Then put him down in his area. If for any reason you can't carry him, snap the leash on quickly and lead him to his spot. Now comes the hard part—hard for you, that is. Just stand there until he urinates and defecates. Move him a few feet in one direction or another if he's just sitting there

TIME TO PLAY!
Playtime can happen both indoors and out. A young puppy is growing so rapidly that he needs sleep more than he needs a lot of physical exercise. Puppies get sufficient exercise on their own just through normal puppy activity. Monitor play with young children so you can remove the puppy when he's had enough, or calm the kids if they get too rowdy. Almost all puppies love to chase after a toy you've thrown, and you can turn your games into educational activities. Every time your puppy brings the toy back to you, say "Give it" (or "Drop it") followed by "Good dog" and throwing it again. If he's reluctant to give it to you, offer a small treat so that he drops the toy as he takes the treat. He will soon get the idea.

BOOT CAMP

Even if one member of the family assumes the role of "drill sergeant," every other member of the family has to know what's involved in the dog's education. Success depends on consistency and knowing what words to use, how to use them, how to say them, when to say them and, most important to the dog, how to praise. The dog will be happy to respond to all members of the family, but don't make the little guy think he's in boot camp!

another ten minutes, or immediately if you see him sniffing and circling. By careful observation, you'll soon work out a successful schedule.

Accidents, by the way, are just that—accidents. Clean them up quickly and thoroughly, without comment, after the puppy has been taken outside to finish his business and then put back into his area or crate. If you witness an accident in progress, say "No!" in a stern voice and get the pup outdoors immediately. No punishment is needed. You and your

A wire pen (called an ex-pen) is easily transported to safely confine your Saluki outdoors when away from home.

Who says we're not people?

canines recognize and accept. Discipline, therefore, is never to be confused with punishment. When you teach your puppy how you want him to behave, and he behaves properly and you praise him for it, you are disciplining him with a form of positive reinforcement.

For a dog, rewards come in the form of praise, a smile, a cheerful tone of voice, a few friendly pats or a rub of the ears. Rewards are also small food treats. Obviously, that does not mean bits of regular dog food. Instead, treats are very small bits of special things like cheese or pieces of soft dog treats. The idea is to reward the dog with some-

puppy are just learning each other's language, and sometimes it's easy to miss a puppy's message. Chalk it up to experience and watch more closely from now on.

KEEPING THE PACK ORDERLY

Discipline is a form of training that brings order to life. For example, military discipline is what allows the soldiers in an army to work as one. Discipline is a form of teaching and, in dogs, is the basis of how the successful pack operates. Each member knows his place in the pack and all respect the leader, or Alpha dog. It is essential for your puppy that you establish this type of relationship, with you as the Alpha, or leader. It is a form of social coexistence that all

WHO'S TRAINING WHOM?

Dog training is a black-and-white exercise. The correct response to a command must be absolute, and the trainer must insist on completely accurate responses from the dog. A trainer cannot command his dog to sit and then settle for the dog's melting into the down position. Often owners are so pleased that their dogs "did something" in response to a command that they just shrug and say, "OK, down" even though they wanted the dog to sit. You want your dog to respond to the command without hesitation: he must respond at that moment and correctly every time.

thing very small that he can taste and swallow, providing instant positive reinforcement. If he has to take time to chew the treat, he will have forgotten what he did to earn it by the time he is finished.

Your puppy should never be physically punished. The displeasure shown on your face and in your voice is sufficient to signal to the pup that he has done something wrong. He wants to please everyone higher up on the social ladder, especially his leader, so a scowl and harsh voice will take care of the error. Growling out the word "Shame!" when the pup is caught in the act of doing something wrong is better than the repetitive "No." Some dogs hear "No" so often that they begin to think it's their name! By the way, do not use the dog's name when you're correcting him. His name is reserved to get his attention for something pleasant about to take place.

There are punishments that have nothing to do with you. For example, your dog may think that chasing cats is one reason for his existence. You can try to stop it as much as you like but without success, because it's such fun for the dog. But one good hissing, spitting swipe of a cat's claws across the dog's nose will put an end to the game forever. Intervene only when your dog's eyeball is seriously at risk. Cat scratches can

Flying straight up for a treat!

cause permanent damage to an innocent but annoying puppy.

When attempting to train a Saluki, as with all of the sighthounds, you must never lose sight of the fact that these dogs are independent, problem-solving, proud dogs. Punishment will never produce an obedient dog. The only way you can work with a Saluki is to convince the dog that the desired behavior is his idea, not yours. Furthermore, Salukis and all of the other sighthounds do not appreciate repetition. Once they have accomplished the desired task, they see no reason to repeat it. Their intelligence is incredible, and one must always remember that this is a "thinking" dog. With that in

PUPPY KINDERGARTEN

COLLAR AND LEASH

Before you begin your Saluki puppy's education, he must be used to his collar and leash. Choose a collar for your puppy that is secure, but not heavy or bulky. He won't enjoy training if he's uncomfortable. A flat buckle collar is fine for everyday wear and for initial puppy training. For older dogs, there are several types of training collars such as the martingale, which is a double loop that tightens slightly around the neck, or the head collar, which is similar to a horse's halter. Do not use a chain choke collar unless you have been specifically shown how to put it on and how to use it. You may not be disposed to use a chain choke collar even if your breeder has told you that it's suitable for your Saluki.

A lightweight 6-foot woven cotton or nylon training leash is preferred by most trainers because it is easy to fold up in your hand and comfortable to hold because there is a certain amount of give to it. There are lessons where the dog will start off 6 feet away from you at the end of the leash. The leash used to take the puppy outside to relieve himself is shorter because you don't want him to roam away from his area. The shorter leash will also be the one to use when you walk the puppy.

mind, we offer the following suggestions for training your Saluki pup. Positive reinforcement will bring great rewards. Punishment of any kind will reap nothing but resentment and refusals. In order to teach your dog anything, you must first get his attention. After all, he cannot learn anything if he is looking away from you with his mind on something else. This can be very trying with sighthounds and with Salukis in particular!

If you've been fortunate enough to enroll in a puppy kindergarten training class, suggestions will be made as to the best collar and leash for your young puppy. I say "fortunate" because your puppy will be in a class with puppies in his age range (up to five months old) of all breeds and sizes. It's the perfect way for him to learn the right way (and the wrong way) to interact with other dogs as well as their people. You cannot teach your puppy how to interpret another dog's sign language. For a first-time puppy owner, these socialization classes are invaluable. For experienced dog owners, they are a real boon to further training.

SMILE WHEN YOU ORDER ME AROUND!

While trainers recommend practicing with your dog every day, it's perfectly acceptable to take a "mental health day" off. It's better not to train the dog on days when you're in a sour mood. Your bad attitude or lack of interest will be sensed by your dog, and he will respond accordingly. Studies show that dogs are well tuned in to their humans' emotions. Be conscious of how you use your voice when talking to your dog. Raising your voice or shouting will only erode your dog's trust in you as his trainer and master.

ATTENTION

You've been using the dog's name since the minute you collected him from the breeder, so you should be able to get his attention by saying his name—with a big smile and in an excited tone of voice. His response will be the puppy equivalent of "Here I am! What are we going to do?" Your immediate response (if you haven't guessed by now) is "Good dog." Rewarding him at the moment he pays attention to you teaches him the proper way to respond when he hears his name.

EXERCISES FOR A BASIC CANINE EDUCATION

THE SIT EXERCISE

There are several ways to teach the puppy to sit. The first one is to catch him whenever he is about to sit and, as his backside nears the floor, say "Sit, good dog!" That's positive reinforcement and, if your timing is sharp, he will learn that what he's doing at that second is connected to your saying "Sit" and that you think he's clever for doing it!

Another method is to start with the puppy on his leash in front of you. Show him a treat in the palm of your right hand. Bring your hand up under his nose and, almost in slow motion, move your hand up and back so his nose goes up in the air and his head tilts back as he follows the treat in your hand. At that point, he will have to either sit or fall over, so as his back legs buckle under, say "Sit, good dog," and then give him the treat and lots of praise. You may have to begin with your hand lightly running up his chest, actu-

READY, SIT, GO!

On your marks, get set: train! Most professional trainers agree that the sit command is the place to start your dog's formal education. Sitting is a natural posture for most dogs, and they respond to the sit exercise willingly and readily. For every lesson, begin with the sit command so that you start out with a successful exercise; likewise, you should practice the sit command at the end of every lesson as well, because you always want to end on a high note.

ally lifting his chin up until he sits. Some (usually older) dogs require gentle pressure on their hindquarters with the left hand, in which case the dog should be on your left side. Puppies generally do not appreciate this physical dominance.

After a few times, you should be able to show the dog a treat in the open palm of your hand, raise your hand waist-high as you say "Sit" and have him sit. Once again, you have taught him two things at the same time. Both the verbal command and the motion of the hand are signals for the sit. Your puppy is watching you almost more than he is listening to you, so what you do is just as important as what you say.

Don't save any of these drills only for training sessions. Use them as much as possible at odd times during a normal day. The dog should always sit before being given his food dish. He should sit to let you go through a doorway first, when the doorbell rings or when you stop to speak to someone on the street.

THE DOWN EXERCISE

Before beginning to teach the down command, you must consider how the dog feels about this exercise. To him, "down" is a submissive position. Being flat on the floor with you standing over him is not his idea of fun. It's up to you to let him know that, while it may not be fun, the reward of your approval is worth his effort.

Start with the puppy on your left side in a sit position. Hold the leash right above his collar in your left hand. Have an extra-special treat, such as a small piece of cooked chicken or hot dog, in your right hand. Place it at the end of the pup's nose and steadily move your hand down and forward along the ground. Hold the leash to prevent a sudden lunge for the food. As the puppy

goes into the down position, say "Down" very gently.

Teaching the down exercise.

The difficulty with this exercise is twofold: it's both the submissive aspect and the fact that most people say the word "Down" as if they were a drill sergeant in charge of recruits! So issue the command sweetly, give him the treat and have the pup maintain the down position for several seconds. If he tries to get up immediately, place your hands on his shoulders and press down gently, giving him a very quiet "Good dog." As you progress with this lesson, increase the "down time" until he will hold it until you say "Okay" (his cue for release). Practice this one in the house at various times throughout the day.

By increasing the length of time during which the dog must maintain the down position,

TIPS FOR TRAINING AND SAFETY

1. Whether on- or off-leash, practice only in a fenced area.
2. Remove the training collar when the training session is over.
3. Don't try to break up a dogfight.
4. "Come," "Leave it" and "Wait" are safety commands.
5. The dog belongs in a crate or behind a barrier when riding in the car.
6. Don't ignore the dog's first sign of aggression. Aggression only gets worse, so take it seriously.
7. Keep the faces of children and dogs separated.
8. Pay attention to what the dog is chewing.
9. Keep the vet's number near your phone.
10. "Okay" is a useful release command.

you'll find many uses for it. For example, he can lie at your feet in the vet's office or anywhere that both of you have to wait, when you are on the phone, while the family is eating and so forth. If you progress to training for competitive obedience, he'll already be all set for the exercise called the "long down."

THE STAY EXERCISE

You can teach your Saluki to stay in the sit, down and stand positions. To teach the sit/stay, have the dog sit on your left side. Hold the leash at waist level in your left hand and let the dog know that you have a treat in your closed right hand. Step forward on your right foot as you say "Stay." Immediately turn and stand directly in front of the dog, keeping your right hand up high so he'll keep his eye on the treat hand and maintain the sit position for a count of five. Return to your original position and offer the reward.

Increase the length of the sit/stay each time until the dog can hold it for at least 30 seconds without moving. After about a week of success, move out on your right foot and take two steps before turning to face the dog. Give the "Stay" hand signal (left palm back toward the dog's head) as you leave. He gets the treat when you return and he holds the sit/stay. Increase the distance that

you walk away from him before turning until you reach the length of your training leash. But don't rush it! Go back to the beginning if he moves before he should. No matter what the lesson, never be upset by having to back up for a few days. The repetition and practice are what will make your dog reliable in these commands. It won't do any good to move on to something more difficult if the command is not mastered at the easier levels. Above all, even if you do get frustrated, never let your puppy know! Always keep a positive, upbeat attitude during training, which will transmit to your dog for positive results.

The down/stay is taught in the same way once the dog is completely reliable and steady with the down command. Again, don't rush it. With the dog in the down position on your left side, step out on your right foot as you say "Stay." Return by walking around in back of the dog and into your original position. While you are training, it's okay to murmur something like "Hold on" to encourage him to stay put. When the dog will stay without moving when you are at a distance of 3 or 4 feet, begin to increase the length of time before you return. Be sure he holds the down on your return until you say "Okay." At that point, he gets his treat—just so he'll remember for next time that it's not over until it's over.

OKAY!

This is the signal that tells your dog that he can quit whatever he was doing. Use "Okay" to end a session on a correct response to a command. (Never end on an incorrect response.) Lots of praise follows. People use "Okay" a lot and it has other uses for dogs, too. Your dog is barking. You say, "Okay! Come!" "Okay" signals him to stop the barking activity and "Come" allows him to come to you for a "Good dog."

THE COME EXERCISE

No command is more important to the safety of your Saluki than "Come." It is what you should say every single time you see the puppy running toward you: "Flash, come! Good dog." During playtime, run a few feet away from the puppy and turn and tell him to "Come" as he is already running to you. You can go so far as to teach your puppy two things at once if you squat down and hold out your arms. As the pup gets close to you and you're saying "Good dog," bring your right arm in about waist high. Now he's also learning the hand signal, an excellent device should you be on the phone when you need to get him to come to you! You'll also both be one step ahead when you enter obedience classes.

Puppies, like children, have notoriously short attention spans, so don't overdo it with any of the training. Keep each lesson short. Break it up with a quick run around the yard or a ball toss, repeat the lesson and quit as soon as the pup gets it right. That way, you will always end with a "Good dog."

When the puppy responds to your well-timed "Come," try it with the puppy on the training leash. This time, catch him off guard, while he's sniffing a leaf or watching a bird: "Flash, come!" You may have to pause for a split second after his name to be sure you have his attention. If the puppy shows any sign of confusion, give the leash a mild jerk and take a couple of steps backward. Do not repeat the command. In this case, you should say "Good come" as he reaches you.

That's the number-one rule of training. Each command word is given just once. Anything more is nagging. You'll also notice that all

In advanced obedience, the dog must retrieve a dumbbell and return it to his owner, building on the foundation of the "Come" command.

commands are one word only. Even when they are actually two words, you say them as one.

Never call the dog to come to you—with or without his name—if you are angry or intend to correct him for some misbehavior. When correcting the pup, you go to him. Your dog must always connect "Come" with something pleasant and with your approval, then you can rely on his response

SHOULD WE ENROLL?

If you have the means and the time, you should definitely take your dog to obedience classes. Begin with Puppy Kindergarten classes in which puppies of all sizes learn basic lessons while getting the opportunity to meet and greet each other; it's as much about socialization as it is about good manners. What you learn in class you can practice at home. And if you goof up in practice, you'll get help in the next session.

(although a 100% "reliable come" is an elusive goal with a sighthound).

Life isn't perfect and neither are puppies. A time will come, often around ten months of age, when he'll become "selectively deaf" or choose to "forget" his name. He may respond by wagging his tail (and even seeming to smile at you) with a look that says "Make me!" Laugh, throw his favorite toy and skip the lesson you had planned. Pups will be pups!

THE HEEL EXERCISE

The second most important command to teach, after the come, is the heel. When you are walking your growing puppy, you need to be in control. Besides, it looks terrible to be pulled and yanked down the street, and it's not much fun either. Your eight-to ten-week-old puppy will probably follow you everywhere, but that's his natural instinct, not your control over the situation. However, any time he does follow you, you can say "Heel" and be ahead of the game, as he will learn to associate this command with the action of following you before you even begin teaching him to heel.

There is a very precise, almost military, procedure for teaching your dog to heel. As with all other obedience training, begin with the dog on your left side. He will be in a very nice sit and you will have the training leash across your chest. Hold the loop and folded leash in your right hand. Pick up the slack leash above the dog in your left hand and hold it loosely at your side. Step out on your left foot as you say "Heel." If the puppy does not move, give a gentle tug or pat your left leg to get him started. If he surges ahead of you, stop and pull him back gently until he is at your side. Tell him to sit and begin again.

Walk a few steps and stop while the puppy is correctly beside you. Tell him to sit and give mild verbal praise. (More enthusiastic praise will encourage him to think the lesson is over.) Repeat the lesson, increasing the number of steps you take only as long as the dog is heeling nicely beside you. When you end the lesson, have him hold the sit and then give him the "Okay" to let him know that this is the end of the lesson. Praise him so that he knows he did a good job.

The cure for excessive pulling (a common problem) is to stop when the dog is no more than 2 or 3 feet ahead of you. Guide him back into position and begin again. With a really determined puller, try switching to a head collar. This will automatically turn the pup's head toward you so you can bring him back easily to the heel position. Give quiet, reassuring praise every time the leash goes slack and he's staying with you.

LET'S GO!

Many people use "Let's go" instead of "Heel" when teaching their dogs to behave on lead. It sounds more like fun! When beginning to teach the heel, whatever command you use, always step off on your left foot. That's the one next to the dog, who is on your left side, in case you've forgotten. Keep a loose leash. When the dog pulls ahead, stop, bring him back and begin again. Use treats to guide him around turns.

Staying and heeling can take a lot out of a dog, so provide play-time and free-running exercise to shake off the stress when the lessons are over. You don't want him to associate training with all work and no fun.

ABOVE: Dog racing is a licensed and closely regulated activity. If you are interested, your local dog club can probably advise you about getting started with your Saluki.

RIGHT: Lure coursing is a popular competition for Salukis and other sighthound breeds, in which their instincts are put to the test. It's amazing to watch the dogs' speed and keen hunting skills.

TRAINING FOR OTHER ACTIVITIES

Once your dog has basic obedience under his collar and is 12 months of age, you can train for competitive obedience or enter the world of agility training. Dogs think agility is pure fun, like being turned loose in an amusement park full of obstacles! There is also tracking, which is open to all "nosey" dogs (which would include all dogs!), and specialized activities geared toward certain types of dogs.

Lure coursing and racing are two activities most suited to a Saluki. There are two types of coursing, open-field coursing and lure coursing, the latter using a plastic bag as a simulated hare. In open-field coursing, the dogs are walked up on the hare in trios and slipped by the huntmaster once the hare is up and running. In lure coursing, the dogs are also slipped in trios, but by the individual owners from a start line over a preset course.

In racing, dogs need to be licensed and then race over shorter courses, usually in groups of four. Various racing and

NO MORE TREATS!

When your dog is responding promptly and correctly to commands, it's time to eliminate treats. Begin by alternating a treat reward with a verbal-praise-only reward. Gradually eliminate all treats while increasing the frequency of praise. Overlook pleading eyes and expectant expressions, but if he's still watching your treat hand, you're on your way to using hand signals.

For those who like to volunteer, there is the wonderful feeling of owning a therapy dog and visiting hospices, nursing homes and veterans' homes to bring smiles, comfort and companionship to those who live there. Around the house, your Saluki can be taught to do some simple chores. You might teach him to carry a basket of household items or to fetch the morning newspaper. The kids can teach the dog all kinds of tricks, from playing hide-and-seek to balancing a biscuit on his nose. A family dog is what rounds out the family. Everything he does, including sitting at your feet and gazing lovingly at you, represents the bonus of owning a dog.

sighthound societies sponsor these events, such as the Large Gazehound Racing Association and the National Oval Track Racing Association.

Salukis resemble gazelles in their effortless jumping ability. Many Salukis compete in agility trials; their innate skills make them naturals at the sport.

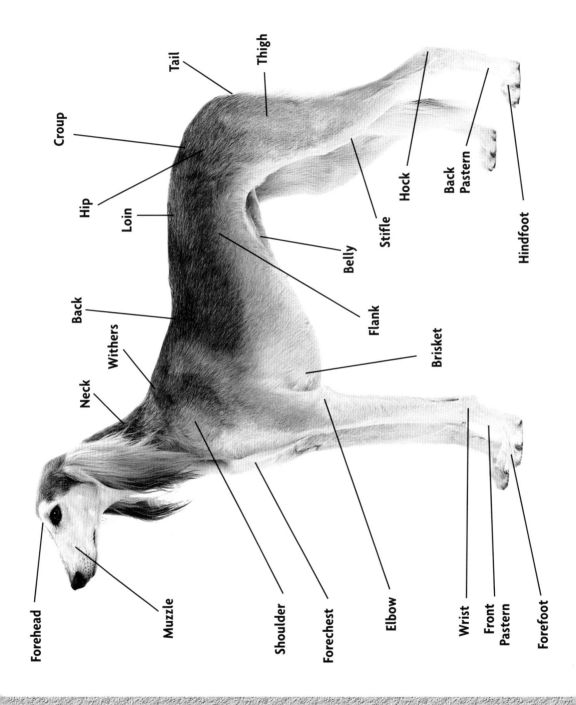

Tail

Thigh

Croup

Hock

Back
Pastern

Hip

Loin

Stifle

Hindfoot

Belly

Back

Flank

Withers

Brisket

Neck

Forehead

Muzzle

Shoulder

Forechest

Elbow

Wrist

Front
Pastern

Forefoot

PHYSICAL STRUCTURE OF THE SALUKI

HEALTHCARE OF YOUR

SALUKI

By Lowell Ackerman DVM, DACVD

HEALTHCARE FOR A LIFETIME
When you own a dog, you become his healthcare advocate over his entire lifespan, as well as being the one to shoulder the financial burden of such care. Accordingly, it is worthwhile to focus on prevention rather than treatment, as you and your pet will both be happier.

Of course, the best place to have begun your program of preventive healthcare is with the initial purchase or adoption of your dog. There is no way of guaranteeing that your new furry friend is free of medical problems, but there are some things you can do to improve your odds. You certainly should have done adequate research into the Saluki and have selected your puppy carefully rather than buying on impulse. Health issues aside, a large number of pet abandonment and relinquishment cases arise from a mismatch between pet needs and owner expectations. This is entirely preventable with appropriate planning and finding a good breeder.

Regarding healthcare issues specifically, it is very difficult to make blanket statements about where to acquire a problem-free pet, but, again, a reputable breeder is your best bet. In an ideal situation you have the opportunity to see both parents, get references from other owners of the breeder's pups and see genetic-testing documentation for several generations of the litter's ancestors. At the very least, you must thoroughly investigate the Saluki and the problems inherent in that breed, as well as the genetic testing available to screen for those problems. Genetic testing offers some important benefits, but testing is available for only a few disorders in a relatively small number of breeds and is not available for some of the most common genetic diseases, such as hip dysplasia, cataracts, epilepsy, cardiomyopathy, etc. This area of research is indeed exciting and increasingly important, and advances will continue to be made each year. In fact, recent research has shown that there is an equivalent dog gene for 75% of

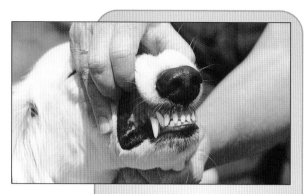

DOGGIE DENTAL DON'TS

A veterinary dental exam is necessary if you notice one or any combination of the following in your dog:

- Broken, loose or missing teeth
- Loss of appetite (which could be due to mouth pain or illness caused by infection)
- Gum abnormalities, including redness, swelling and bleeding
- Drooling, with or without blood
- Yellowing of the teeth or gumline, indicating tartar
- Bad breath

Dental devices for dogs make it easy for owners to care for their dog's teeth. Use only toothpaste formulated for dogs, not products made for humans.

known human genes, so research done in either species is likely to benefit the other.

We've also discussed that evaluating the behavioral nature of

your Saluki and that of his immediate family members is an important part of the selection process that cannot be underestimated or overemphasized. It is sometimes difficult to evaluate temperament in puppies because certain behavioral tendencies, such as some forms of aggression, may not be immediately evident. More dogs are euthanized each year for behavioral reasons than for all medical conditions combined, so it is critical to take temperament issues seriously. Start with a well-balanced, friendly companion and put the time and effort into proper socialization, and you will both be rewarded with a lifelong valued relationship.

Assuming that you have started off with a pup from healthy, sound stock, you then become responsible for helping your veterinarian keep your pet healthy. Some crucial things happen before you even bring your puppy home. Parasite control typically begins at two weeks of age, and vaccinations typically begin at six to eight weeks of age. A pre-pubertal evaluation is typically scheduled for about six months of age. At this time, a dental evaluation is done (since the adult teeth are now in), heartworm prevention is started and neutering or spaying is most commonly done.

It is critical to commence regular dental care at home if you

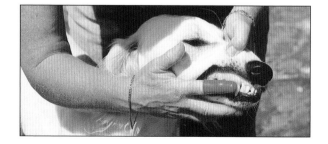

have not already done so. It may not sound very important, but most dogs have active periodontal disease by four years of age if they don't have their teeth cleaned regularly at home, not just at their veterinary exams. Dental problems lead to more than just bad "doggy breath." Gum disease can have very serious medical consequences. If you start brushing your dog's teeth and using antiseptic rinses from a young age, your dog will be accustomed to it and will not resist. The results will be healthy dentition, which your pet will need to enjoy a long, healthy life.

Most dogs are considered adults at a year of age, although some larger breeds still have some filling out to do up to about two or so years old. Even individual dogs within each breed have different healthcare requirements, so work with your veterinarian to determine what will be needed and what your role should be. This doctor-client relationship is important, because as vaccination guidelines change, there may not be an annual "vaccine visit" scheduled. You must make sure that you see your veterinarian at least annually, even if no vaccines are due, because this is the best opportunity to coordinate healthcare activities and to make sure that no medical issues creep by unaddressed.

TAKING YOUR DOG'S TEMPERATURE

It is important to know how to take your dog's temperature at times when you think he may be ill. It's not the most enjoyable task, but it can be done without too much difficulty. It's easier with a helper, preferably someone with whom the dog is friendly, so that one of you can hold the dog while the other inserts the thermometer.

Before inserting the thermometer, coat the end with petroleum jelly. Insert the thermometer slowly and gently into the dog's rectum about one inch. Wait for the reading, about two minutes. Be sure to remove the thermometer carefully and clean it thoroughly after each use.

A dog's normal body temperature is between 100.5 and 102.5 degrees F. Immediate veterinary attention is required if the dog's temperature is below 99 or above 104 degrees F.

When your Saluki reaches three-quarters of his anticipated lifespan, he is considered a "senior" and likely requires some special care. In general, if you've

YOUR DOG NEEDS TO VISIT THE VET IF:

- He has ingested a toxin such as antifreeze or a toxic plant; in these cases, administer first aid and call the vet right away
- His teeth are discolored, loose or missing or he has sores or other signs of infection or abnormality in the mouth
- He has been vomiting, has had diarrhea or has been constipated for over 24 hours; call immediately if you notice blood
- He has refused food for over 24 hours
- His eating habits, water intake or toilet habits have noticeably changed; if you have noticed weight gain or weight loss
- He shows symptoms of bloat, which requires *immediate* attention
- He is salivating excessively
- He has a lump in his throat
- He has lumps or bumps anywhere on the body
- He is very lethargic
- He appears to be in pain or otherwise has trouble chewing or swallowing
- His skin loses elasticity

    Of course, there will be other instances in which a visit to the vet is necessary; these are just some of the signs that could be indicative of serious problems that need to be caught as early as possible.

been taking great care of your canine companion throughout his formative and adult years, the transition to senior status should be a smooth one. Age is not a disease, and as long as everything is functioning as it should, there is no reason why most of late adulthood should not be rewarding for both you and your pet. This is especially true if you have tended to the details, such as regular veterinary visits, proper dental care, excellent nutrition and management of bone and joint issues.

At this stage in your Saluki's life, your veterinarian will want to schedule visits twice yearly, instead of once, to run some laboratory screenings, electrocardiograms and the like, and to change the diet to something more digestible. Catching problems early is the best way to manage them effectively. Treating the early stages of heart disease is so much easier than trying to intervene when there is more significant damage to the heart muscle. Similarly, managing the beginning of kidney problems is fairly routine if there is no significant kidney damage. Other problems, like cognitive dysfunction (similar to senility and Alzheimer's disease), cancer, diabetes and arthritis, are more common in older dogs, but all can be treated to help the dog live as many happy, comfortable years as possible. Just as in people, medical management is more effective (and less expensive) when you catch things early.

SELECTING A VETERINARIAN

Everyone has his own idea about what to look for in a vet, an individual who will play a big role in his dog's (and, of course, his own) life for many years to come. For some, it is the compassionate caregiver with whom they hope to develop a professional relationship to span the lifetime of their dogs and even their future pets. For others, they are seeking a clinician with keen diagnostic and therapeutic insight who can deliver state-of-the-art healthcare. Still others need a veterinary facility that is open evenings and weekends, is in close proximity or provides mobile veterinary services to accommodate their schedules; these people may not much mind that their dogs might see different veterinarians on each visit. Just as we have different reasons for selecting our own healthcare professionals (e.g., covered by insurance plan, expert in field, convenient location, etc.), we should not expect that there is a one-size-fits-all recommendation for selecting a veterinarian and veterinary practice. The best advice is to be honest in your assessment of what you expect from a veterinary practice and to conscientiously research the

YOUR PUPPY AND THE VET
This first visit should establish a rapport between you, your puppy and the vet. Regular vaccination programs usually begin when the puppy is eight weeks old, so you want to be sure that the monthly visits are a positive interaction with the personnel in the hospital. Also remember that socialization of the pup occurs primarily between 8 and 16 weeks, so contact with children, the postman, other dogs, other animals and the vet are highly beneficial. Lack of socialization at this critical time can lead to serious behavioral problems later in life. Happy experiences at the vet as a pup will produce a dog that never fears visiting his doctor.

The puppy should have his teeth examined and his skeletal conformation and general health checked prior to sale, and a certificate should be issued by the veterinarian. Male Saluki puppies may have undescended testicles as young pups, but in most cases the testes do descend before the dog is a year old. If you encounter behavioral problems, your veterinarian may have training in temperament evaluation or can recommend a canine behaviorist.

options in your area. You will quickly appreciate that not all veterinary practices are the same, and you will be happiest with one that truly meets your needs.

There is another point to be considered in the selection of veterinary services. Not that long ago, a single veterinarian would attempt to manage all medical and surgical issues as they arose. That was often problematic, because veterinarians are trained in many species and many diseases, and it was just impossible for general veterinary practitioners to be experts in every species, every field and every ailment. However, just as in the human healthcare fields, specialization has allowed general practitioners to concentrate on primary healthcare delivery, especially wellness and the prevention of infectious diseases, and to utilize a network of specialists to assist in the management of conditions that require specific expertise and experience. Thus there are now many types of veterinary specialists, including dermatologists, cardiologists, ophthalmologists, surgeons, internists, oncologists, neurologists, behaviorists, criticalists and others to help primary-care veterinarians deal with complicated medical challenges. In most cases, specialists see cases referred by primary-care veterinarians, make diagnoses and set up management plans. From there, the animals' ongoing care is returned to their primary-care veterinarians. This important team approach to your pet's medical-care needs has provided opportunities for advanced care and an unparalleled level of quality to be delivered. Further, as many maladies are not treated in the same manner, second opinions can be valuable.

With all of the opportunities for your Saluki to receive high-quality veterinary medical care, there is another topic that needs to be addressed at the same time—cost. It's been said that you can have excellent healthcare or inexpensive healthcare, but never both; this is as true in veterinary medicine as it is in human medicine. While veterinary costs are a fraction of what the same services cost in the human healthcare arena, it is still difficult to deal with unanticipated medical costs, especially since they can easily creep into hundreds or even thousands of dollars if specialists or emergency services become involved. However, there are

Gently clean the outer surface of the ears with a swab dipped in baby oil. Do not probe down into the ear.

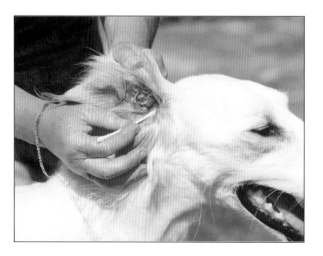

The Eyes Have It!

Eye disease is more prevalent among dogs than most people think, ranging from slight infections that are easily treated to serious complications that can lead to permanent sight loss. Eye diseases need veterinary attention in their early stages to prevent irreparable damage. This list provides descriptions of some common eye diseases:

Cataracts: Symptoms are white or gray discoloration of the eye lens and pupil, which causes fuzzy or completely obscured vision. Surgical treatment is required to remove the damaged lens and replace it with an artificial one.

Conjunctivitis: An inflammation of the mucous membrane that lines the eye socket, leaving the eyes red and puffy with excessive discharge. This condition is easily treated with antibiotics.

Corneal damage: The cornea is the transparent covering of the iris and pupil. Injuries are difficult to detect but manifest themselves in surface abnormality, redness, pain and discharge. Most infections of the cornea are treated with antibiotics and require immediate medical attention.

Dry eye: This condition is caused by deficient production of tears that lubricate and protect the eye surface. A telltale sign is yellow-green discharge. Left undiagnosed, your dog will experience considerable pain, infections and possibly blindness. Dry eye is commonly treated with antibiotics, although more advanced cases may require surgery.

Glaucoma: This is caused by excessive fluid pressure in the eye. Symptoms are red eyes, gray or blue discoloration, pain, enlarged eyeballs and loss of vision. Antibiotics sometimes help, but surgery may be needed.

ways of managing these risks. The easiest is to buy pet health insurance and realize that its foremost purpose is not to cover routine healthcare visits but rather to serve as an umbrella for those rainy days when your pet needs medical care and you don't want to worry about whether or not you can afford that care. Read and understand exactly what is and is not covered under each policy that you consider. Pet health insurance is not always cost-effective.

VACCINATIONS AND INFECTIOUS DISEASES

There has never been an easier time to prevent a variety of infectious diseases in your dog, but the advances we've made in veterinary medicine come with a price—choice. Now while it may seem that this choice is a good thing (and it is), it has never

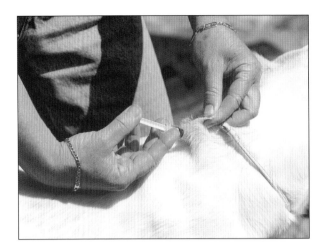

necessary to reevaluate the situation and deal with some tough questions. It is important to realize that whether or not to use a particular vaccine depends on the

Your vet will advise you about vaccination boosters for your adult Saluki.

been more difficult for the pet owner (or the veterinarian) to make an informed decision about the best way to protect pets through vaccination.

Years ago, it was just accepted that puppies got a starter series of vaccinations and then annual "boosters" throughout their lives to keep them protected. As more and more vaccines became available, consumers wanted the convenience of having all of that protection in a single injection. The result was "multivalent" vaccines that crammed a lot of protection into a single syringe. The manufacturers' recommendations were to give the vaccines annually, and this was a simple enough protocol to follow. However, as veterinary medicine has become more sophisticated and we have started looking more at healthcare quandaries rather than convenience, it became

SALUKI SYMPTOMS

Salukis are remarkably free of skin disorders, since they are smooth-coated and do not have deep wrinkles. The most common clinical sign, hair loss or sparse hair, is not actually a skin disease, but an indication of hypothyroidism. If you notice hair loss or large bare patches, your dog should be tested for thyroid function. Excess protein in the diet can cause sparse hair, particularly on the underbelly and the legs. Simply reducing the dog's protein intake will normally correct this. Allergies can cause skin and coat problems. If the allergen is in the dog's food, a veterinary diet is often quite helpful. If a dog develops hives, this could be a reaction to a bee sting or the bite of a spider or insect.

Auto-immune conditions are commonly referred to as being allergic to yourself, while allergies are usually inflammatory reactions to outside stimuli. Auto-immune diseases cause serious damage to the tissues that are involved. These diseases have been on the rise in recent years in Salukis, perhaps because of the small gene pool and the practice of using one "famous" stud dog to sire many litters.

COMMON INFECTIOUS DISEASES

Let's discuss some of the diseases that create the need for vaccination in the first place. Following are the major canine infectious diseases and a simple explanation of each.

Rabies: A devastating viral disease that can be fatal in dogs and people. In fact, vaccination of dogs and cats is an important public-health measure to create a resistant animal buffer population to protect people from contracting the disease. Vaccination schedules are determined on a government level and are not optional for pet owners; rabies vaccination is required by law in all 50 states.

Parvovirus: A severe, potentially life-threatening disease that is easily transmitted between dogs. There are four strains of the virus, but it is believed that there is significant "cross-protection" between strains that may be included in individual vaccines.

Distemper: A potentially severe and life-threatening disease with a relatively high risk of exposure, especially in certain regions. In very high-risk distemper environments, young pups may be vaccinated with human measles vaccine, a related virus that offers cross-protection when administered at four to ten weeks of age.

Hepatitis: Caused by canine adenovirus type 1 (CAV-1), but since vaccination with the causative virus has a higher rate of adverse effects, cross-protection is derived from the use of adenovirus type 2 (CAV-2), a cause of respiratory disease and one of the potential causes of canine cough. Vaccination with CAV-2 provides long-term immunity against hepatitis, but relatively less protection against respiratory infection.

Canine cough: Also called tracheobronchitis, actually a fairly complicated result of viral and bacterial offenders; therefore, even with vaccination, protection is incomplete. Wherever dogs congregate, canine cough will likely be spread among them. Intranasal vaccination with *Bordetella* and parainfluenza is the best safeguard, but the duration of immunity does not appear to be very long, typically a year at most. These are non-core vaccines, but vaccination is sometimes mandated by boarding kennels, obedience classes, dog shows and other places where dogs congregate to try to minimize spread of infection.

Leptospirosis: A potentially fatal disease that is more common in some geographic regions. It is capable of being spread to humans. The disease varies with the individual "serovar," or strain, of *Leptospira* involved. Since there does not appear to be much cross-protection between serovars, protection is only as good as the likelihood that the serovar in the vaccine is the same as the one in the pet's local environment. Problems with *Leptospira* vaccines are that protection does not last very long, side effects are not uncommon and a large percentage of dogs (perhaps 30%) may not respond to vaccination.

Borrelia burgdorferi: The cause of Lyme disease, the risk of which varies with the geographic area in which the pet lives and travels. Lyme disease is spread by deer ticks in the eastern US and western black-legged ticks in the western part of the country, and the risk of exposure is high in some regions. Lameness, fever and inappetence are most commonly seen in affected dogs. The extent of protection from the vaccine has not been conclusively demonstrated.

Coronavirus: This disease has a high risk of exposure, especially in areas where dogs congregate, but it typically causes only mild to moderate digestive upset (diarrhea, vomiting, etc.). Vaccines are available, but the duration of protection is believed to be relatively short and the effectiveness of the vaccine in preventing infection is considered low.

There are many other vaccinations available, including those for *Giardia* and canine adenovirus-1. While there may be some specific indications for their use, and local risk factors to be considered, they are not widely recommended for most dogs.

risk of contracting the disease against which it protects, the severity of the disease if it is contracted, the duration of immunity provided by the vaccine, the safety of the product and the needs of the individual animal. In a very general sense, rabies, distemper, hepatitis and parvovirus are considered core vaccine needs, while parainfluenza, *Bordetella bronchiseptica*, leptospirosis, coronavirus and borreliosis (Lyme disease) are considered non-core needs and best reserved for animals that demonstrate reasonable risk of contracting the diseases.

Kennel cough is often included in routine vaccination, but this is often not as effective as the nasal spray and neither injection nor spray confers the same level of immunity as for other major diseases.

The first vaccination should occur at 8 weeks and continue every 30 days until 16 weeks. Maternal interference with antibody production lasts up to 16 weeks, so continuing the vaccination schedule is critical to ensure the pup is properly protected. With all vaccinations, schedules and booster shots, you must take your breeder's and vet's advice.

NEUTERING/SPAYING

Sterilization procedures (neutering for males/spaying for females) are meant to accomplish

HEARTWORM ZONE

Although heartworm cases have been reported in all 48 continental states, the largest threat exists in the Southeast and Mississippi River Valley. The following states have the highest risk factors: Texas, Florida, Louisiana, North Carolina, Georgia, Mississippi, Tennessee, South Carolina, Alabama and Indiana. Discuss the risk factor with your veterinarian to determine your course of prevention for your dog.

several purposes. While the underlying premise is to address the risk of pet overpopulation, there are also some medical and behavioral benefits to the surgeries as well. For females, spaying prior to the first estrus (heat cycle) leads to a marked reduction in the risk of mammary cancer. There also will be no manifestations of "heat" to attract male dogs and no bleeding in the house. For males, there is prevention of testicular cancer and a reduction in the risk of prostate problems. In both sexes, there may be some limited reduction in sex drive and aggressive behaviors toward other dogs, and some diminishing of urine marking, roaming and mounting.

While neutering and spaying do indeed prevent animals from contributing to pet overpopulation, even no-cost and low-cost neutering options have not eliminated the problem. Perhaps one of the main reasons for this is that individuals that intentionally breed their dogs and those that allow their animals to run at large are the main causes of unwanted offspring. Also, animals in shelters are often there because they were abandoned or relinquished, not because they came from unplanned matings. Neutering/spaying is important, but it should be considered in the context of the real causes of animals' ending up in shelters and eventually being euthanized.

BEST TIME TO SPAY

In bitches, besides eliminating the possibility of pregnancy, spaying very significantly reduces the risk of breast cancer, from about 30% to less than 1%. If the bitch is not spayed prior to her first season (estrus), any benefit in preventing breast cancer is eliminated, increasing the incidence to as high a level as an unspayed bitch. In an American study (1995) by Schneider *et al*, reported in the *Journal of the National Cancer Institute*, the actual data are presented. Many Saluki bitches do not come into season until 12 to 14 months of age, although individuals may come into season as early as 8 months. Therefore, careful monitoring and family history are important in determining when to spay.

One of the important considerations regarding neutering is that it is a surgical procedure. This sometimes gets lost in discussions of low-cost procedures and commoditization of the process. In females, spaying is specifically referred to as an ovariohysterectomy. In this procedure, a midline incision is made in the abdomen and the entire uterus and both ovaries are surgically removed. While this is a major invasive surgical procedure, it usually has few complications, because it is typically performed on healthy young animals. However, it is major surgery, as any woman who has had a hysterectomy will attest.

In males, neutering has traditionally referred to castration, which involves the surgical removal of both testicles. While still a significant piece of surgery, there is not the abdominal exposure that is required in the female surgery. In addition, there is now a chemical sterilization option, in which a solution is injected into each testicle, leading to atrophy of the sperm-producing cells. This can typically be done under sedation rather than full anesthesia. This is a relatively new approach, and there are no long-term clinical studies yet available.

Neutering/spaying is typically done around 6 months of age at most veterinary hospitals, although large breeds normally wait until 9–12 months old.

A scanning electron micrograph of a dog flea, *Ctenocephalides canis*, on dog hair.

EXTERNAL PARASITES

FLEAS

Fleas have been around for millions of years and, while we have better tools now for controlling them than at any time in the past, there still is little chance that they will end up on an endangered species list. Actually, they are very well adapted to living on our pets, and they continue to adapt as we make advances.

The female flea can consume 15 times her weight in blood during active reproduction and can lay as many as 40 eggs a day. These eggs are very resistant to the effects of insecticides. They hatch into larvae, which then mature and spin cocoons. The immature fleas reside in this pupal stage until the time is right for feeding. This pupal stage is also very resistant to the effects of insecticides, and pupae can last in the environment without feeding for many months. Newly emergent fleas are attracted to animals by the warmth of the animals' bodies, movement and exhaled carbon dioxide. However, when they first emerge from their cocoons, they orient towards light; thus when an animal passes between a flea and the light source, casting a shadow, the flea pounces and starts to feed. If the animal turns out to be a dog or cat, the reproductive cycle continues. If the flea lands on another type of animal, including a person, the flea will bite but will then look for a more appropriate host. An emerging adult flea can survive without feeding for up to 12 months but, once it tastes blood, it can survive off its host for only three to four days.

It was once thought that fleas spend most of their lives in the environment, but we now know that fleas won't willingly jump off a dog unless leaping to another dog or when physically removed by brushing, bathing or other manipulation. Flea eggs, on the other hand, are shiny and smooth, and they roll off the animal and into the environment. The eggs, larvae and pupae then exist in the environment, but once the adult finds a susceptible animal, it's home sweet home until the flea is forced to seek refuge elsewhere.

Since adult fleas live on the animal and immature forms survive in the environment, a successful treatment plan must address all stages of the flea life cycle. There are now several safe and effective flea-control products that can be applied on a monthly

> ## FLEA PREVENTION FOR YOUR DOG
> - Discuss with your veterinarian the safest product to protect your dog, likely in the form of a monthly tablet or a liquid preparation placed on the back of the dog's neck.
> - For dogs suffering from flea-bite dermatitis, a shampoo or topical insecticide treatment is required.
> - Your lawn and property should be sprayed with an insecticide designed to kill fleas and ticks that lurk outdoors.
> - Using a flea comb, check the dog's coat regularly for any signs of parasites.
> - Practice good housekeeping. Vacuum floors, carpets and furniture regularly, especially in the areas that the dog frequents, and wash the dog's bedding weekly.
> - Follow up house-cleaning with carpet shampoos and sprays to rid the house of fleas at all stages of development. Insect growth regulators are the safest option.

basis. These include fipronil, imidacloprid, selamectin and permethrin (found in several formulations). Most of these products have significant flea-killing rates within 24 hours. However, none of them will control the immature forms in the environment. To accomplish this, there are a variety of insect growth regulators that can be sprayed into

THE FLEA'S LIFE CYCLE

What came first, the flea or the egg? This age-old mystery is more difficult to comprehend than the actual cycle of the flea. Fleas usually live only about four months. A female can lay 2,000 eggs in her lifetime.

Photo by Carolina Biological Supply Co.

Egg

After ten days of rolling around your carpet or under your furniture, the eggs hatch into larvae, which feed on various and sundry debris. In days or months, depending on the climate, the larvae spin cocoons and develop into the pupal or nymph stage, which quickly develop into fleas.

Larva

Photo by Carolina Biological Supply Co.

Pupa

These immature fleas must locate a host within 10 to 14 days or they will die. Only about 1% of the flea population exist as adult fleas, while the other 99% exist as eggs, larvae or pupae.

KILL FLEAS THE NATURAL WAY

If you choose not to go the route of conventional medication, there are some natural ways to ward off fleas:

- Dust your dog with a natural flea powder, composed of such herbal goodies as rosemary, wormwood, pennyroyal, citronella, rue, tobacco powder and eucalyptus.
- Apply diatomaceous earth, the fossilized remains of single-cell algae, to your carpets, furniture and pet's bedding. Even though it's not good for dogs, it's even worse for fleas, which will dry up swiftly and die.
- Brush your dog frequently, give him adequate exercise and let him fast occasionally. All of these activities strengthen the dog's system and make him more resistant to disease and parasites.
- Bathe your dog with a capful of pennyroyal or eucalyptus oil.
- Feed a natural diet, free of additives and preservatives. Add some fresh garlic and brewer's yeast to the dog's morning portion, as these items have flea-repelling properties.

the environment (e.g., pyriproxyfen, methoprene, fenoxycarb) as well as insect development inhibitors such as lufenuron that can be administered. These compounds have no effect on adult fleas, but they stop immature forms from developing into adults. In years gone by we relied heavily on toxic insecticides (such as organophosphates, organochlorines and carbamates) to manage the flea problem, but today's options are not only much safer to use on our pets but also safer for the environment.

TICKS

Ticks are members of the spider class (arachnids) and are blood-sucking parasites capable of transmitting a variety of diseases, including Lyme disease, ehrlichiosis, babesiosis and Rocky Mountain spotted fever. It's easy to see ticks on your own skin, but it is more of a challenge when your furry companion is affected. Whenever you happen to be planning a stroll in a tick-infested area (especially forests, grassy or wooded areas or parks) be prepared to do a thorough inspection of your dog afterward to search for ticks. Ticks can be tricky, so make sure you spend time looking in the ears, between the toes and everywhere else where a tick might hide. Ticks need to be attached for 24–72 hours before they transmit most of the diseases that they carry, so you do have a window of opportunity for some preventive intervention.

A TICKING BOMB

There is nothing good about a tick's harpooning his nose into your dog's skin. Among the diseases caused by ticks are Rocky Mountain spotted fever, canine ehrlichiosis, canine babesiosis, canine hepatozoonosis and Lyme disease. If a dog is allergic to the saliva of a female wood tick, he can develop tick paralysis.

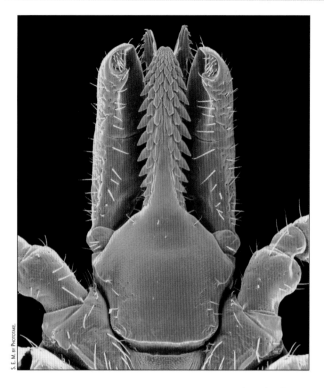

S. E. M. BY PHOTOTAKE.

A scanning electron micrograph of the head of a female deer tick, *Ixodes dammini*, a parasitic tick that carries Lyme disease.

Female ticks live to eat and breed. They can lay between 4,000 and 5,000 eggs and they die soon after. Males, on the other hand, live only to mate with the females and continue the process as long as they are able. Most ticks live on multiple hosts before parasitizing dogs. The immature forms typically reside on grass and shrubs, waiting for susceptible animals to walk by. The larvae and nymph stages typically feed on wildlife.

If only a few ticks are present on a dog, they can be plucked out, but it is important to remove the entire head and mouthparts,

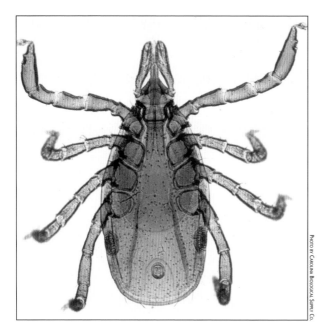

Deer tick,
Ixodes dammini.

PHOTO BY CAROLINA BIOLOGICAL SUPPLY CO.

which may be deeply embedded in the skin. This is best accomplished with forceps designed especially for this purpose; fingers can be used but should be protected with rubber gloves, plastic wrap or at least a paper towel. The tick should be grasped as closely as possible to the animal's skin and should be pulled upward with steady, even pressure. Do not squeeze, crush or puncture the body of the tick or you risk exposure to any disease carried by that tick. Once the ticks have been removed, the sites of attachment should be disinfected. Your hands should then be washed with soap and water to further minimize risk of contagion. The tick should be disposed of in a container of alcohol or household bleach.

Some of the newer flea products, specifically those with fipronil, selamectin and permethrin, have effect against some, but not all, species of tick. Flea collars containing appropriate pesticides (e.g., propoxur, chlorfenvinphos) can aid in tick control. In most areas, such collars should be placed on animals in March, at the beginning of the tick season, and changed regularly. Leaving the collar on when the pesticide level is waning invites the development of resistance. Amitraz collars are also good for tick control, and the active ingredient does not interfere with other flea-control products. The ingredient helps prevent the attachment of ticks to the skin and will cause those ticks already on the skin to detach themselves.

TICK CONTROL

Removal of underbrush and leaf litter and the thinning of trees in areas where tick control is desired are recommended. These actions remove the cover and food sources for small animals that serve as hosts for ticks. With continued mowing of grasses in these areas, the probability of ticks' surviving is further reduced. A variety of insecticide ingredients (e.g., resmethrin, carbaryl, permethrin, chlorpyrifos, dioxathion and allethrin) are registered for tick control around the home.

MITES

Mites are tiny arachnid parasites that parasitize the skin of dogs. Skin diseases caused by mites are referred to as "mange," and there are many different forms seen in dogs. These forms are very different from one another, each one warranting an individual description.

Sarcoptic mange, or scabies, is one of the itchiest conditions that affects dogs. The microscopic *Sarcoptes* mites burrow into the superficial layers of the skin and can drive dogs crazy with itchiness. They are also communicable to people, although they can't complete their reproductive cycle on people. In addition to being tiny, the mites also are often difficult to find when trying to make a diagnosis. Skin scrapings from multiple areas are examined microscopically but, even then, sometimes the mites cannot be found.

Fortunately, scabies is relatively easy to treat, and there are a variety of products that will successfully kill the mites. Since the mites can't live in the environment for very long without feeding, a complete cure is usually possible within four to eight weeks.

Cheyletiellosis is caused by a relatively large mite, which sometimes can be seen even without a microscope. Often referred to as "walking dandruff," this also causes itching, but not usually as profound as with scabies. While *Cheyletiella* mites

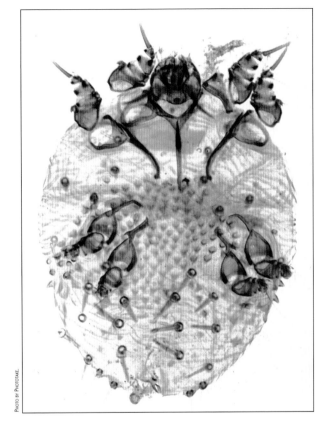

PHOTO BY PHOTOTAKE.

Sarcoptes scabiei, commonly known as the "itch mite."

can survive somewhat longer in the environment than scabies mites, they too are relatively easy to treat, being responsive to not only the medications used to treat scabies but also often to flea-control products.

Otodectes cynotis is the canine ear mite and is one of the more common causes of mange, especially in young dogs in shelters or pet stores. That's because the mites are typically present in large numbers and are quickly spread to nearby animals. The mites rarely do

S. E. M. BY DR. DENNIS KUNKEL, UNIVERSITY OF HAWAII.

Micrograph of a dog louse, *Heterodoxus spiniger*. Female lice attach their eggs to the hairs of the dog. As the eggs hatch, the larval lice bite and feed on the blood. Lice can also feed on dead skin and hair. This feeding activity can cause hair loss and skin problems.

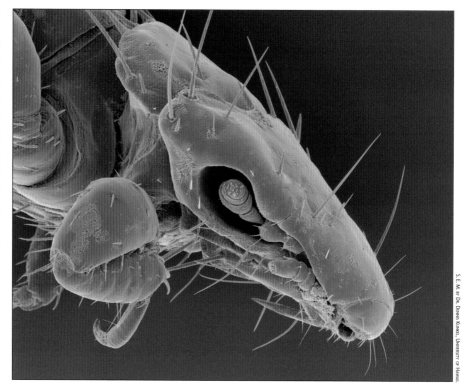

much harm but can be difficult to eradicate if the treatment regimen is not comprehensive. While many try to treat the condition with ear drops only, this is the most common cause of treatment failure. Ear drops cause the mites to simply move out of the ears and as far away as possible (usually to the base of the tail) until the insecticide levels in the ears drop to an acceptable level—then it's back to business as usual! The successful treatment of ear mites requires treating all animals in the household with a systemic insecticide, such as selamectin, or a combination of miticidal ear drops combined with whole-body flea-control preparations.

Demodicosis, sometimes referred to as red mange, can be one of the most difficult forms of mange to treat. Part of the problem has to do with the fact that the mites live in the hair follicles and they are relatively well shielded from topical and systemic products. The main issue, however, is that demodectic mange typically results only when there is some underlying process interfering with the dog's immune system.

Since *Demodex* mites are normal residents of the skin of

mammals, including humans, there is usually a mite population explosion only when the immune system fails to keep the number of mites in check. In young animals, the immune deficit may be transient or may reflect an actual inherited immune problem. In older animals, demodicosis is usually seen only when there is another disease hampering the immune system, such as diabetes, cancer, thyroid problems or the use of immune-suppressing drugs. Accordingly, treatment involves not only trying to kill the mange mites but also discerning what is interfering with immune function and correcting it if possible.

Chiggers represent several different species of mite that don't parasitize dogs specifically, but do latch on to passersby and can cause irritation. The problem is most prevalent in wooded areas in the late summer and fall. Treatment is not difficult, as the mites do not complete their life cycle on dogs and are susceptible to a variety of miticidal products.

Mosquitoes

Mosquitoes have long been known to transmit a variety of diseases to people, as well as just being biting pests during warm weather. They also pose a real risk to pets. Not only

do they carry deadly heartworms but recently there also has been much concern over their involvement with West Nile virus. While we can avoid heartworm with the use of preventive medications, there are no such preventives for West Nile virus. The only method of prevention in endemic areas is active mosquito control. Fortunately, most dogs that have been exposed to the virus only developed flu-like symptoms and, to date, there have not been the large number of reported deaths in canines as seen in some other species.

Illustration of *Demodex folliculoram*.

MOSQUITO REPELLENT

Low concentrations of DEET (less than 10%), found in many human mosquito repellents, have been safely used in dogs but, in these concentrations, probably give only about two hours of protection. DEET may be safe in these small concentrations, but since it is not licensed for use on dogs, there is no research proving its safety for dogs. Products containing permethrin give the longest-lasting protection, perhaps two to four weeks. As DEET is not licensed for use on dogs, and both DEET and permethrin can be quite toxic to cats, appropriate care should be exercised. Other products, such as those containing oil of citronella, also have some mosquito-repellent activity, but typically have a relatively short duration of action.

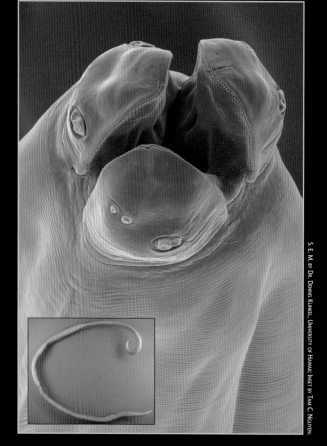

S. E. M. BY DR. DENNIS KUNKEL, UNIVERSITY OF HAWAII. INSET BY TAM C. NGUYEN.

The ascarid roundworm *Toxocara canis,* showing the mouth with three lips. INSET: Photomicrograph of the roundworm *Ascaris lumbricoides.*

INTERNAL PARASITES: WORMS

ASCARIDS

Ascarids are intestinal round-worms that rarely cause severe disease in dogs. Nonetheless, they are of major public health significance because they can be transferred to people. Sadly, it is children who are most commonly affected by the parasite, probably from inadvertently ingesting ascarid-contaminated soil. In fact, many yards and children's sand-boxes contain appreciable numbers of ascarid eggs. So, while ascarids don't bite dogs or latch onto their intestines to suck blood, they do cause some nasty medical conditions in children and are best eradicated from our furry friends. Because pups can start passing ascarid eggs by three weeks of age, most parasite-control programs begin at two weeks of age and are repeated every two weeks until pups are eight weeks old. It is important to

S. E. M. BY DR. DENNIS KUNKEL, UNIVERSITY OF HAWAII.

realize that bitches can pass ascarids to their pups even if they test negative prior to whelping. Accordingly, bitches are best treated at the same time as the pups.

HOOKWORMS

Unlike ascarids, hookworms do latch onto a dog's intestinal tract and can cause significant loss of blood and protein. Similar to ascarids, hookworms can be transmitted to humans, where they cause a condition known as cutaneous larval migrans. Dogs can become infected either by consuming the infective larvae or by the larvae's penetrating the skin directly. People most often get infected when they are lying on the ground (such as on a beach) and the larvae penetrate the skin. Yes, the larvae can penetrate through a beach blanket. Hookworms are typically susceptible to the same medications used to treat ascarids.

The hookworm *Ancylostoma caninum* infests the intestines of dogs. INSET: Note the row of hooks at the posterior end, used to anchor the worm to the intestinal wall.

WHIPWORMS

Whipworms latch onto the lower aspects of the dog's colon and can cause cramping and diarrhea. Eggs do not start to appear in the dog's feces until about three months after the dog was infected. This worm has a peculiar life cycle, which makes it more difficult to control than ascarids or hookworms. The good thing is that whipworms rarely are transferred to people.

Some of the medications used to treat ascarids and hookworms are also effective against whipworms, but, in general, a separate treatment protocol is needed. Since most of the medications are effective against the adults but not the eggs or larvae, treatment is typically repeated in three weeks, and then often in three

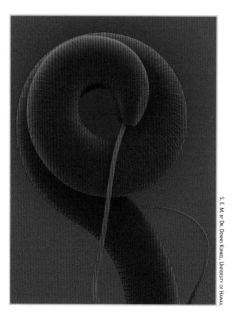

Adult whipworm, *Trichuris* sp., an intestinal parasite.

S. E. M. BY DR. DENNIS KUNKEL, UNIVERSITY OF HAWAII.

WORM-CONTROL GUIDELINES
- Practice sanitary habits with your dog and home.
- Clean up after your dog and don't let him sniff or eat other dogs' droppings.
- Control insects and fleas in the dog's environment. Fleas, lice, cockroaches, beetles, mice and rats can act as hosts for various worms.
- Prevent dogs from eating uncooked meat, raw poultry and dead animals.
- Keep dogs and children from playing in sand and soil.
- Kennel dogs on cement or gravel; avoid dirt runs.
- Administer heartworm preventives regularly.
- Have your vet examine your dog's stools at your annual visits.
- Select a boarding kennel carefully so as to avoid contamination from other dogs or an unsanitary environment.
- Prevent dogs from roaming. Obey local leash laws.

months as well. Unfortunately, since dogs don't develop resistance to whipworms, it is difficult to prevent them from getting reinfected if they visit soil contaminated with whipworm eggs.

TAPEWORMS

There are many different species of tapeworm that affect dogs, but *Dipylidium caninum* is probably the most common and is spread by fleas. Flea larvae feed on organic debris and tapeworm eggs in the environment and, when a dog chews at himself and manages to ingest fleas, he might get a dose of tapeworm at the same time. The tapeworm then develops further in the intestine of the dog.

The tapeworm itself, which is a parasitic flatworm that latches onto the intestinal wall, is composed of numerous segments. When the segments break off into the intestine (as proglottids), they may accumulate around the rectum, like grains of rice. While this tapeworm is disgusting in its behavior, it is not directly communicable to humans (although humans can also get infected by swallowing fleas).

A much more dangerous flatworm is *Echinococcus multilocularis*, which is typically found in foxes, coyotes and wolves. The eggs are passed in the feces and infect rodents, and, when dogs eat the rodents, the dogs can be infected by thousands of adult tapeworms. While the parasites don't cause many problems in dogs, this is considered the most lethal worm infection that people can get. Take appropriate precautions if you live in an area in which these tapeworms are found. Do not use mulch that may contain feces of dogs, cats or wildlife, and discourage your pets from hunting wildlife. Treat these tapeworm infections aggressively in pets, because if humans get infected, approximately half die.

HEARTWORMS

Heartworm disease is caused by the parasite *Dirofilaria immitis* and is seen in dogs around the world. A member of the roundworm group, it is spread between dogs by the bite of an infected mosquito. The mosquito injects infective larvae into the dog's skin with its bite, and these larvae develop under the skin for a period of time before making their way to the heart. There they develop into adults, which grow and create blockages of the heart, lungs and major blood vessels there. They also start producing offspring (microfilariae)

A dog tapeworm proglottid (body segment).

The dog tapeworm *Taenia pisiformis*.

A Look at Internal Parasites

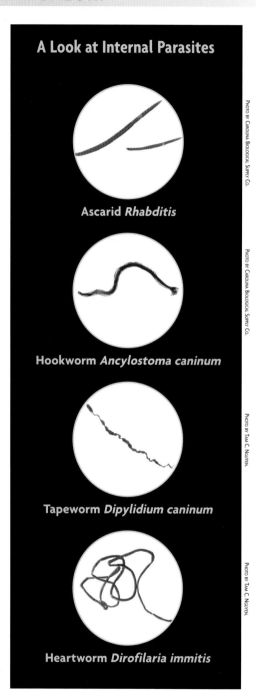

Ascarid *Rhabditis*

Hookworm *Ancylostoma caninum*

Tapeworm *Dipylidium caninum*

Heartworm *Dirofilaria immitis*

and these microfilariae circulate in the bloodstream, waiting to hitch a ride when the next mosquito bites. Once in the mosquito, the microfilariae develop into infective larvae and the entire process is repeated.

When dogs get infected with heartworm, over time they tend to develop symptoms associated with heart disease, such as coughing, exercise intolerance and potentially many other manifestations. Diagnosis is confirmed by either seeing the microfilariae themselves in blood samples or using immunologic tests (antigen testing) to identify the presence of adult heartworms. Since antigen tests measure the presence of adult heartworms and microfilarial tests measure offspring produced by adults, neither are positive until six to seven months after the initial infection. However, the beginning of damage can occur by fifth-stage larvae as early as three months after infection. Thus it is possible for dogs to be harboring problem-causing larvae for up to three months before either type of test would identify an infection.

The good news is that there are great protocols available for preventing heartworm in dogs. Testing is critical in the process, and it is important to understand the benefits as well as the limitations of such testing. All dogs six months of age or older that have not been on continuous heartworm-preventive medication should be

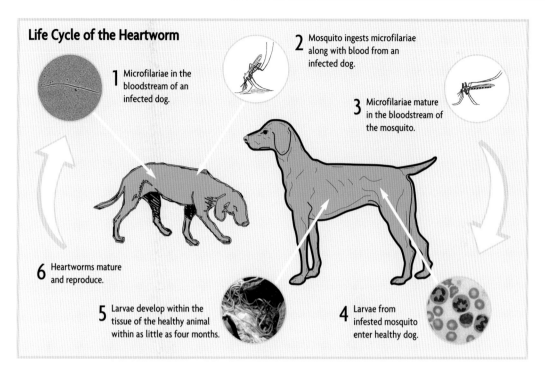

Life Cycle of the Heartworm

1 Microfilariae in the bloodstream of an infected dog.

2 Mosquito ingests microfilariae along with blood from an infected dog.

3 Microfilariae mature in the bloodstream of the mosquito.

4 Larvae from infested mosquito enter healthy dog.

5 Larvae develop within the tissue of the healthy animal within as little as four months.

6 Heartworms mature and reproduce.

screened with microfilarial or antigen tests. For dogs receiving preventive medication, periodic antigen testing helps assess the effectiveness of the preventives. The American Heartworm Society guidelines suggest that annual retesting may not be necessary when owners have absolutely provided continuous heartworm prevention. Retesting on a two- to three-year interval may be sufficient in these cases. However, your veterinarian will likely have specific guidelines under which heartworm preventives will be prescribed, and many prefer to err on the side of safety and retest annually.

It is indeed fortunate that heartworm is relatively easy to prevent, because treatments can be as life-threatening as the disease itself. Treatment requires a two-step process that kills the adult heartworms first and then the microfilariae. Prevention is obviously preferable; this involves a once-monthly oral or topical treatment. The most common oral preventives include ivermectin (not suitable for some breeds), moxidectin and milbemycin oxime; the once-a-month topical drug selamectin provides heartworm protection in addition to flea, tick and other parasite controls.

SHOWING YOUR
SALUKI

Conformation judging is a hands-on task, as the judge examines the Saluki's overall structure.

Is dog showing in your blood? Are you excited by the idea of gaiting your handsome Saluki around the ring to the thunderous applause of an enthusiastic audience? Are you certain that your beloved Saluki is flawless? If this sounds like you, and if you are considering entering your Saluki in a dog show, here are some basic questions to ask yourself:

- Did you purchase a "show-quality" puppy from the breeder?
- Is your puppy at least six months of age?
- Does the puppy exhibit correct show type for his breed?
- Does your puppy have any disqualifying faults?
- Is your Saluki registered with the American Kennel Club?

- How much time do you have to devote to training, grooming, conditioning and exhibiting?
- Do you understand the rules and regulations of a dog show?
- Do you have time to learn how to show your dog properly?
- Do you have the financial resources to invest in showing your dog?
- Will you show the dog yourself or hire a professional handler?
- Do you have a vehicle that can accommodate your weekend trips to the dog shows?

Success in the show ring requires more than a pretty face, a waggy tail and a pocketful of liver. Even though dog shows can be exciting and enjoyable, the sport of conformation makes great demands on the exhibitors and the dogs. Very few novices, even those with good dogs, will find themselves in the winners' circle, though it does happen. Don't be disheartened, though. Every exhibitor began as a novice and worked his way up to the Group ring. It's the "working your way up" part that you must keep in mind.

Assuming that you have purchased a puppy of the correct type and quality for showing, let's begin to examine the world of showing and what's required to get started. Although the entry fee into a dog show is nominal, there are lots of other hidden costs involved with "finishing" your Saluki, that is, making him a champion. Things like equipment, travel, training and conditioning all cost money. A more serious campaign will include fees for a professional handler, boarding, cross-country travel and advertising. Top-winning show dogs can represent a very considerable investment—over $100,000 has been spent in campaigning some dogs. (The investment can be less, of course, for owners who don't use professional handlers.)

Many owners, on the other hand, enter their "average" Salukis in dog shows for the fun and enjoyment of it. Dog showing makes an absorbing hobby, with many rewards for dogs and owners alike. If you're having fun, meeting other people who share your interests and enjoying the overall experience, you likely will catch the "bug." Once the dog-show bug bites, its effects can last a lifetime! Soon you will be envisioning yourself in the center ring at the Westminster Kennel Club Dog Show in New York City, competing for the prestigious Best in Show cup.

CONFORMATION BASICS
Visiting a dog show as a spectator is a great place to start. Pick up the show catalog to find out what time your breed is being shown, who is judging the breed and in which ring the classes will be held. To start, Salukis compete against other Salukis, and the winner is selected as Best of Breed by the judge. This is the procedure for each breed. At a group show, all of the Best of Breed winners go on to compete for Group One in their respective groups. For example, all Best of Breed winners in a given group compete against each other; this is done for all seven groups. Finally, all seven group winners go head to head in the ring for the Best in Show award.

What most spectators don't understand is the basic idea of conformation. A dog show is often referred as a "conformation" show. This means that the judge should decide how each dog stacks up (conforms) to the breed standard for his given breed: how well does this Saluki conform to the ideal representative detailed in the stan-

AKC GROUPS
For showing purposes, the American Kennel Club divides its recognized breeds into seven groups: Hounds, Sporting Dogs, Working Dogs, Terriers, Toys, Non-Sporting Dogs and Herding Dogs. The Saluki is in the Hound Group.

dard? Ideally, this is what happens. In reality, however, this ideal often gets slighted as the judge compares Saluki #1 to Saluki #2. Again, the ideal is that each dog is judged based on his merits in comparison to his breed standard, not in comparison to the other dogs in the ring. It is easier for judges to compare dogs of the same breed to decide which they think is the better specimen; in the Group and Best in Show ring, however, it is very difficult to compare one breed to another, like apples to oranges. Thus the dog's conformation to the breed standard—not to mention

advertising dollars and good handling—is essential to success in conformation shows. The dog described in the standard (the standard for each AKC breed is written and approved by the breed's national parent club and then submitted to the AKC for approval) is the perfect dog of that breed, and breeders keep their eye on the standard when they choose which dogs to breed, hoping to get closer and closer to the ideal with each litter.

Another good first step for the novice is to join a dog club. You will be astonished by the many and different kinds of dog clubs in the country, with about 5,000 clubs holding events every year. Perhaps you've made some friends visiting a show held by a particular club and you would like to join that club. Dog clubs may specialize in a single breed, like a local or regional Saluki club, or in a specific pursuit, such as obedience, tracking or coursing. There are all-breed clubs for all dog enthusiasts; they sponsor special training days, seminars on topics like grooming or handling or lectures on breeding or canine genetics. There are also clubs that specialize in certain types of dogs, like sighthounds, hunting dogs, companion dogs, etc.

A parent club is the national organization, sanctioned by the AKC, which promotes and safeguards its breed in the country. The Saluki Club of America was

MEET THE AKC

The American Kennel Club is the main governing body of the dog sport in the United States. Founded in 1884, the AKC consists of 500 or more independent dog clubs plus 4,500 affiliated clubs, all of which follow the AKC rules and regulations. Additionally, the AKC maintains a registry for pure-bred dogs in the US and works to preserve the integrity of the sport and its continuation in the country. Over 1,000,000 dogs are registered each year, representing about 150 recognized breeds. There are over 15,000 competitive events held annually for which over 2,000,000 dogs enter to participate. Dogs compete to earn over 40 different titles, from Champion to Companion Dog to Master Agility Champion.

formed in 1924 and can be contacted on the Internet at www.salukiclub.org. The parent club holds an annual national specialty show, usually in a different city each year, in which many of the country's top dogs, handlers and breeders gather to compete. At a specialty show, only members of a single breed are invited to participate. There are also group specialties, in which all members of a group are invited. For more information about dog clubs and events in your area, contact the AKC at www.akc.org or write them at their Raleigh, NC address.

OTHER TYPES OF COMPETITION
In addition to conformation shows, the AKC holds a variety of other competitive events.

BECOMING A CHAMPION
An official AKC championship of record requires that a dog accumulate 15 points under three different judges, including two "majors" under different judges. Points are awarded based on the number of dogs entered into competition, varying from breed to breed and place to place. A win of three, four or five points is considered a "major." The AKC annually assigns a schedule of points to adjust to the variations that accompany a breed's popularity and the population of a given area.

Examining the shoulder and neck insertion for correct conformation.

Obedience trials, agility trials and tracking trials are open to all breeds, while hunting tests, field trials, lure coursing, herding tests and trials, earthdog tests and coonhound events are limited to specific breeds or groups of breeds. The Junior Showmanship program is offered to aspiring young handlers and their dogs, and the Canine Good Citizen® program is an all-around good-behavior test open to all dogs, pure-bred and mixed.

OBEDIENCE TRIALS
Mrs. Helen Whitehouse Walker, a Standard Poodle fancier, can be credited with introducing obedience trials to the United States. In the 1930s she designed a series of exercises based on those of the Associated Sheep, Police, Army Dog Society of Great Britain. These exercises were intended to evaluate the working

relationship between dog and owner. Since those early days of the sport in the US, obedience trials have grown more and more popular, and now more than 2,000 trials each year attract over 100,000 dogs and their owners. Any dog registered with the AKC, regardless of neutering or other

ON THE MOVE

The truest test of a dog's proper structure is his gait, the way the dog moves. The American Kennel Club defines gait as "the pattern of footsteps at various rates of speed, each pattern distinguished by a particular rhythm and footfall." That the dog moves smoothly and effortlessly indicates to the judge that the dog's structure is well made.

disqualifications that would preclude entry in conformation competition, can participate in obedience trials.

There are three levels of difficulty in obedience competition. The first (and easiest) level is the Novice, in which dogs can earn the Companion Dog (CD) title. The intermediate level is the Open level, in which the Companion Dog Excellent (CDX) title is awarded. The advanced level is the Utility level, in which dogs compete for the Utility Dog (UD) title. Classes at each level are further divided into "A" and "B," with "A" for beginners and "B" for those with more experience. In order to win a title at a given level, a dog must earn three "legs." A "leg" is accomplished when a dog scores 170 or higher (200 is a perfect score). The scoring system gets a little trickier when you understand that a dog must score more than 50% of the points available for each exercise in order to actually earn the points. Available points for each exercise range between 20 and 40.

Once he's earned the UD title, a dog can go on to win the prestigious title of Utility Dog Excellent (UDX) by winning "legs" in ten shows. Additionally, Utility Dogs who win "legs" in Open B and Utility B earn points toward the lofty title of Obedience Trial Champion (OTCh.). Established in 1977 by the AKC, this title requires a dog to earn 100 points as well as three first places in a combination of Open B and Utility B classes under three different judges. The "brass ring" of obedience competition is the AKC's National Obedience Invitational. This is an exclusive competition for only the cream of the obedience crop. In order to qualify for the invitational, a dog must be ranked in either the top 25 all-breeds in obedience or in the top three for his breed in obedience. The title at stake here is that of National Obedience Champion (NOC).

AGILITY TRIALS

Agility trials became sanctioned by the AKC in August 1994, when the first licensed agility trials were held. Since that time, agility certainly has grown in popularity by leaps and bounds, literally! The AKC allows all registered breeds (including Miscellaneous Class breeds) to participate, providing the dog is 12 months of age or older. Agility is designed so that the handler demonstrates how well the dog can work at his side. The handler directs his dog through, over, under and around an obstacle course that includes jumps, tires, the dog walk, weave poles, pipe tunnels, collapsed tunnels and more. While working his way through the course, the dog must keep one eye and ear on the handler and the rest of his

Success! From conformation to agility to sighthound events, the Saluki has the opportunity to participate and fare well in many areas of the dog sport.

body on the course. The handler runs along with the dog, giving verbal and hand signals to guide the dog through the course.

The first organization to promote agility trials in the US was the United States Dog Agility Association, Inc. (USDAA). Established in 1986, the USDAA sparked the formation of many member clubs around the country. To participate in USDAA trials, dogs must be at least 18 months of age. The USDAA and AKC both offer titles to winning dogs, although the exercises and requirements of the two organizations differ. You should join a local agility club to learn more about the sport.

LURE COURSING

Owners of sighthound breeds have the opportunity to participate in lure coursing. Lure-coursing events are exciting and fast-paced, requiring dogs to follow an artificial lure around a course on an open field. Scores are based on the dog's speed, enthusiasm, agility, endurance and ability to follow the lure. At the non-competitive level, lure coursing is designed to gauge a sighthound's instinctive coursing ability. Competitive lure coursing is more demanding, requiring training and conditioning for a dog to develop his coursing instincts and skills to the fullest, thus preserving the intended function of all sighthound breeds.

Lure coursing is certainly wonderful physical and mental exercise for a dog. A dog must be at least one year of age to enter an AKC coursing event, and he must not have any disqualifications according to his breed standard. Check the AKC's rules and regulations for details. To get started, you can consult the AKC's website to help you find a coursing club in your area. A club can introduce you to the sport and help you learn how to train your dog correctly.

Titles awarded in lure coursing are Junior Courser (JC), Senior Courser (SC) and Master Courser (MC); these are suffix titles, affixed to the end of the dog's name. The Field Champion (FC) title is a prefix title, affixed to the beginning of the dog's name. A Dual Champion is a hound that has earned both a Field Champion title as well as a show championship. A Triple Champion (TC) title is awarded to a dog that is a Champion, Field Champion and Obedience Trial Champion. The suffix Lure Courser Excellent (LCX) is given to a dog who has earned the FC title plus 45 additional championship points, and number designations are added to the title upon each additional 45 championship points earned (LCX II, III, IV and so on).

Sighthounds also can participate in events sponsored by the American Sighthound Field Association (ASFA), an organization devoted to the pursuit of lure coursing. The ASFA was founded in 1972 as a means of keeping open field coursing dogs fit in the off-season. It has grown into the largest lure-coursing association in the world. Dogs must be of an accepted sighthound breed in order to be eligible for participation. Each dog must pass a certification run in which he shows that he can run with another dog without interfering.

The course is laid out using pulleys and a motor to drive the string around the pulleys. Normally white plastic bags are used as lures, although real fur strips may also be attached. Dogs run in trios, each handled by their own slipper. The dogs are scored on their endurance, follow, speed, agility and enthusiasm. Dogs earn their Field Champion titles by earning two first places, or one first- and two second-place finishes, as well as accumulating 100 points. They can then go on to earn the LCM title, Lure Courser of Merit, by winning four first places and accumulating 300 additional points.

OPEN-FIELD COURSING

Salukis were originally used as coursing dogs, hunting in wide-open spaces, often accompanied by a falcon, while the human hunters followed on foot or on horseback. Fortunately, some Saluki owners live in areas of the world where they can still course their hounds, though falconry is illegal in many countries. Sadly, coursing the Saluki in Great Britain may soon be a thing of the past, although the adherents of

Up and over! Navigating an obstacle in an agility trial.

open-field coursing are still trying to petition Parliament to reverse their decision.

In the US, open-field coursing is available primarily in California, Idaho, Colorado, Wyoming and New Mexico. Open-field coursing is regulated by the National Open Field Coursing Association (CA and NM) and by the North American Coursing Association (CO, WY, and ID).

To participate in open-field coursing, your Saluki must be in exceptional condition, have great prey drive and be able to work all day in extreme weather conditions. The same goes for you, the handler, it must be said.

If you are seriously interested in open-field coursing, take your pup on regular visits to open fields where he can learn about natural barriers, obstacles and changes in terrain. At the same time, he is building a solid, strong

TRACKING

Tracking tests are exciting ways to test your Saluki's instinctive scenting ability on a competitive level. All dogs have a nose, and all breeds are welcome in tracking tests. The first AKC-licensed tracking test took place in 1937 as part of the Utility level at an obedience trial, and thus competitive tracking was officially begun. The first title, Tracking Dog (TD), was offered in 1947, ten years after the first official tracking test. It was not until 1980 that the AKC added the title Tracking Dog Excellent (TDX), which was followed by the title Versatile Surface Tracking (VST) in 1995. Champion Tracker (CT) is awarded to a dog who has earned all three of those titles.

In lure coursing, the dog chases an artificial lure and is judged on different points, including speed and enthusiasm.

body and learning to return to you on his own. If you are starting with an older dog, he must be in good health and weight. You will need to work him slowly into the condition needed to be able to run all day. Typical courses are one to two miles in length; each dog is expected to run this distance at full speed and return, prepared to do it again.

White- and black-tailed jackrabbits are the main prey hunted in the US. Ideal terrain is vast open areas of flat or slightly rolling fields, with natural cover sufficient to provide cover for the jackrabbits, yet open enough to allow a good view of the course. In the US, this is available mostly in the western states.

The hunt begins when the huntmaster calls for the three dogs in the course, followed by the gallery (the dogs and handlers not in the course being called). The huntmaster and hunt dogs (with their handlers) start out a few steps, then the gallery steps out, strung in a line behind the hunt-master and hunt dogs, shoulder to shoulder. When a jackrabbit is sighted and the huntmaster judges it to be coursable, he checks to see if at least one of the hunt dogs is sighted. If so, he calls the Tally-Ho.

The dogs then are released to course the jackrabbit. The judges have to move with the dogs so they can see the course. More often than not, the jackrabbit escapes and the dogs are called back. Judging is based on a scale of points and usually only one dog from each preliminary course advances to the finals. If there are too few jackrabbits to complete the meet, as often happens, the meet is called when darkness comes or the weather closes in.

Open-field coursing is not for the out-of-condition show dog or the faint of heart. Those who participate believe with every fiber of their being that it is the only way to preserve the intelligence, grace, stamina and hunting abilities of the Saluki. Breeders whose dogs participate in this activity will have dogs of exceptional quality, if the performance Saluki is the dog you are seeking.

RACING

The Large Gazehound Racing Association (LGRA) and the National Oval Track Racing Association (NOTRA) are organizations that sponsor and regulate dog races. Races are usually either 200-yard sprints (LGRA) or semi- or complete ovals (NOTRA). Both of these organizations allow most sighthound breeds except Whippets to participate. (Whippets have their own racing organizations exclusively for the breed.) In both LGRA and NOTRA races, the dogs generally run out of starting boxes, meaning that racing dogs must be trained to the box. Local racing clubs offer training programs that can assist novice owners and dogs.

Dogs compete in a draw of four each and are ranked according to their previous racing record. The lure in LGRA events consists of both real fur and a

Born to run, the Saluki delights in any kind of running sport, especially relishing open-field coursing and racing.

predator call. In NOTRA events, the lure is white plastic and often a fur strip. There are three programs and the dogs are rotated through the draw according to their finish in each preceding program. Dogs earn the Gazehound Racing Champion (GRC) or the Oval Racing Champion (ORC) title when they accumulate 15 race points. Dogs can go on to earn the Superior titles by accumulating 30 additional points.

Both LGRA and NOTRA races are owner-participation sports, in which each owner plays some role: catcher, walker, line judge or foul judge. If you plan to race your dog, plan to work all day during a race day! There is little time for anything else, but the reward of seeing four dogs pour over the finish line shoulder to shoulder is more than enough.

FOR MORE INFORMATION....

For reliable up-to-date information about registration, dog shows and other canine competitions, contact one of the national registries by mail or via the Internet.

American Kennel Club
5580 Centerview Dr., Raleigh, NC 27606-3390
www.akc.org

United Kennel Club
100 E. Kilgore Road, Kalamazoo, MI 49002
www.ukcdogs.com

Canadian Kennel Club
89 Skyway Ave., Suite 100, Etobicoke, Ontario
M9W 6R4 Canada
www.ckc.ca

INDEX

*Page numbers in **boldface** indicate illustrations.*

My Saluki

PUT YOUR PUPPY'S FIRST PICTURE HERE

Dog's Name _____

Date _____ Photographer _____